CityPack
Los Angeles

EMMA STANFORD

Emma Stanford's first visit to LA was as a teenager: she discovered Disneyland and Gap jeans. Since then her LaLaland explorations (both touristic and sartorial) have clocked up many thousands of freeway miles, several wild spending sprees and an insider knowledge to rival most Angelenos. She loves her sea and sun and has written AA Explorer Hawaii *and* Explorer Florida.

City and surroundings map continues on inside back cover

AA Publishing

Contents

About this book

KEY TO SYMBOLS

✚ map reference on the fold-out map accompanying this book (see below)

✉ address

☎ telephone number

🕐 opening times

🍴 restaurant or café on premises or nearby

Ⓜ nearest Metro (underground) train station

🚉 nearest overground train station

🚌 nearest bus route

⛴ nearest riverboat or ferry stop

♿ facilities for visitors with disabilities

✋ admission charge

↔ other nearby places of interest

❓ tours, lectures or special events

➤ cross-reference (see below)

ℹ tourist information

CityPack Los Angeles is divided into six sections to cover the most important aspects of your visit to Los Angeles. It includes:

- An overview of the city and its people
- Itineraries, walks and excursions
- The top 25 sights to visit
- Features about different aspects of the city that make it special
- Detailed listings of restaurants, hotels, shops and nightlife
- Practical information

In addition, easy-to-read text boxes provide fascinating extra facts and snippets, highlights of places to visit and invaluable practical advice.

CROSS-REFERENCES

To help you make the most of your visit, cross-references, indicated by ➤ , show you where to find additional information about a place or subject.

MAPS

The fold-out map in the wallet at the back of the book is a comprehensive street plan of central Los Angeles. All map references in this book refer to this map. For example, the Natural History Museum, 900 Exposition Boulevard has the following information: ✚ J11 indicating the grid square of the map in which the Natural History Museum will be found.

The city-centre maps found on the inside front and back covers of the book itself are for quick reference. They show Los Angeles and its surrounding area, and the Top 25 Sights, described on pages 24–48, are clearly plotted here by number (**1** – **25**, not page number) from west to east across the city.

PRICES

An indication of the admission charge (for all attractions) is given by categorising the standard adult rate as follows:

Expensive (over $10), Moderate (over $5) and Inexpensive (under $5).

LOS ANGELES *life*

INTRODUCING LOS ANGELES

Welcome to LaLaLand! A land of sunshine, promise and wealth beyond the dreams of avarice. Squeezed into a 1,000-square-mile basin encircled by picturesque mountains and the Pacific Ocean, this vast urban megalopolis is home to movie stars and Mickey Mouse, richly endowed art museums and scantily clad beachcombers. LA (locals never spell out 'Los Angeles') is balanced on the cutting edge of cool, where restaurants, cars, pets and people blister in and out of fashion in the blink of an eye. Tinseltown is also a master of illusion with a pedigree stretching back to the dawn of the Hollywood movie era, when D W Griffith's 1915 *Birth of a Nation* revolutionised the city's burgeoning film industry. Behind the palm trees and the power lunches, there are earthquakes, crime, mud slides and grinding poverty – all part of the deal, and they lend LA an uncompromising edge.

Despite all that, the statistical likelihood of being caught in a major earthquake is remote. You are far more likely to suffer financially from valet parking, a legalised form of daylight robbery in a city that is landscaped by the combustion engine, where it seems everybody drives everywhere. Though driving is certainly the easiest way to get around LA, don't forget that the city's 500 miles of freeway hell clog up by 7AM, and freeway mayhem also reigns again from 3 until 7PM. The average commuter here drives a 30-mile round trip daily, checking local radio stations for traffic information, up-to-date weather conditions and (in summer) the all-important smog report.

First-time visitors can't help but notice the urban sprawl that distinguishes LA from other American cities (including San Francisco, its rival to the north)

Driving

Angelenos drive fast, change lanes more often than their socks and cultivate a complete disregard for other traffic sharing the road. Nonetheless, the best way to get around LA is by car. It's not as scary as it may seem. Plan your trip in advance, leave plenty of time, and avoid rush hour periods and 'car pool' lanes unless you have the requisite number of passengers.

Mural at Venice Beach

Downtown Los Angeles, backed by the San Gabriel Mountains

that boast a strong centralised city flavour. But decentralisation was evident early on in LA, as newcomers were consistently drawn to the city's mild climate, new opportunities and cheap real estate. Los Angeles changed dramatcially in a period of 50 years, as growth industries like film, oil and aircraft turned a town that was relatively uninhabited in the early 1880s into the fifth-largest city in America by 1930, with a growing population soaring above 1.2 million people. Today Los Angeles County comprises a whopping six area telephone codes and a mighty 16 million inhabitants.

Since 1781, when LA was founded by missionary farmers, Downtown area has moved only a couple of blocks from the original site. The trolley car system that once connected surrounding cities to Downtown has, of course, been replaced by a maze of freeways, but Downtown remains the hub of the city, a highrise corporate ghetto where all eyes are focused on the emerging Pacific Rim market over the horizon. Beyond Downtown is Los Angeles County, made up of 88 incorporated cities and dozens of individual neighbourhoods. On paper, it all looks like a cultural melting pot with the largest Hispanic and Asian/Pacific populations, and fourth largest African-American population in the United States. In reality, many neighbourhoods are anything but a melting pot, and racial and ethnic tensions are always just below the surface.

Literary LA

There is no better place to read Raymond Chandler's dark, gritty crime novels than in the city that inspired them in the 1930s and 1940s. Evelyn Waugh's satirical look at the American way of death, *The Loved One*, is based on LA's Forest Lawn Cemetery; Nathanael West rips into early Hollywood in *Day of the Locust*; and Hollywood insider and producer Julia Phillips lays bare 'the industry' in modern times with *You'll Never Eat Lunch in This Town Again*.

TGIF

Weekends in LA begin on a Friday night when Westwood Village goes pedestrian to cope with crowds sauntering between pavement cafés, cinemas and record shops. Santa Monica's Third Street Promenade is another hot spot. Saturday is for shopping (➤ 70–77) and grooming (➤ 83) before the Big Night Out at Club… On Sunday mornings, brunch at the beach is an institution in the South Bay area, and no first-time visitor to LA should miss the colourful street parade that is Venice Beach each weekend.

Cut a broad swath west of Downtown to the Pacific shore at Santa Monica, and you will find the majority of the city's top sightseeing attractions, shopping, dining and entertainment opportunities. Hollywood, West Hollywood, Beverly Hills and West LA are the fickle heart of LaLaLand, where star-struck celebrities come out at night to watch each other in Spago or the Sky Bar, at the Sunset Room, or the Improv. Of course, if you go and look for them, they are never there. You may have better luck with star-sightings while window-shopping along Montana or Sunset Plaza, but the only way you can be sure of spotting celebrities in Tinseltown is to get a ticket for the *Tonight Show*.

However, if genuine stars are in short supply, there is nothing to prevent you from hamming it up in a dozen familiar-from-the-big- (or small-) screen locations, from Union Station (*Blade Runner*) and the Griffith Park Observatory (*Rebel without a Cause*) to Malibu (*Baywatch*, *The Rockford Files*). LA is definitely the place to indulge fantasies. Hire a limo for an evening out, wear sunglasses around the clock, hobnob with Goofy at Disneyland and dress up for win-dow shopping in Beverly Hills, then flounce into the Regent Beverly Wilshire (the *Pretty Woman* hotel) for a cocktail. Vistors who prefer culture to celebrities should know that LA has become a world-class player in the visual arts, with top-notch collec-tions at several venues in the city, such as the Getty. Santa Monica or Century City are favourite spots to catch dinner and a first-run movie; or you can check out the theatre and con-cert listings in the free *LA Weekly*.

Taking the dog for a walk, Venice Beach style

LOS ANGELES IN FIGURES

Distances from Downtown
- Distance from San Francisco: 397 miles
- Distance from New York: 2,767 miles
- Distance from London: 5,460 miles
- Distance from San Andreas fault: 33 miles

Area & population
- City of Los Angeles: 467 square miles/3.8 million people
- Los Angeles Five County Area: 34,149 square miles/16 million people
- Number of incorporated cities in the Five County Area: 88

Geography
- Latitude: 34° 04'N; longitude: 118° 15'W (roughly that of Atlanta, Casablanca, Beirut, Kashmir and Osaka)
- Highest point: Mt. Wilson, 5,710 feet
- Lowest point: sea level
- Miles of shoreline in Five County Area: 160
- Miles of freeway: 528.3

Weather
- Warmest in July–August (average 84°/64°F, 29°/18°C, max/min)
- Coolest in January (average 68°/48°F, 20°/9°C, max/min)
- Wettest in January
- Average days of sunshine per annum: 329 (90 per cent)
- Smog season: May–October
- LA's last snow fell in January 1962 (½ inch)

Entertainment & Attractions
- An average 50 productions are filmed daily on LA streets (► 52 Entertainment Industry Development Corporation)
- 1,100 LA theatre productions sell 4 million tickets annually
- LA's film and TV industry employs 150,000 people
- More artists, writers, filmmakers, actors, dancers and musicians live and work in LA than in any other city at any other time in the history of civilisation
- Annual movie industry receipts around $19 billion
- LA County's No. 1 attraction: Universal Studios (Disneyland is No. 2, No. 1 in Orange County)

A CHRONOLOGY

Pre-1781	Indian village of Yang-Na near Los Angeles River, close to present-day site of City Hall. Mission of San Gabriel Archangel founded 1771 in San Gabriel Valley (➤ 12).
1781	*Los Pobladores*, 44 farmer-settlers from the San Gabriel mission, establish El Pueblo de Nuestra Señora la Reina de Los Angeles in the fertile Los Angeles basin.
1818	The Avila Adobe house is built for cattle rancher and mayor Don Francisco Avila.
1825	California becomes a territory of Mexico.
1842	Gold is discovered in the San Fernando Valley, six years before the discovery at Sutter's Mill that triggered the Gold Rush.
1848	End of the Mexican–American War. California becomes part of the United States. (Achieves statehood 1850).
1872	The Southern Pacific Railroad Company commissions the first guidebook to Southern California. Charles Nordhoff's *California: For Health, Pleasure and Residence* creates a flood of visitors to the area.
1876	The first transcontinental railroad (Southern Pacific) arrives in Los Angeles.
1880	The University of Southern California is founded with 53 students and 12 teachers.
1881	General Harrison Gray Otis publishes the first issue of the *Los Angeles Times*.
1882	The city's first African-American community is established at 1st and Los Angeles streets.
1892	Edward Doheny discovers oil in Downtown.
1902	Los Angeles' first movie house, the Electric Theater, opens on Main Street. Rose Parade is founded.

1909 Santa Monica Pier opens to attract tourists.

1911 The Nestor Co establishes Hollywood's first movie studio in the former Blondeau Tavern at Sunset and Gower.

1913 Cecil B De Mille makes Hollywood's first full-length feature film, *The Squaw Man*.

1919 United Artists Film Corp founded by D W Griffith, Mary Pickford, Douglas Fairbanks and Charlie Chaplin to improve actors' pay and working conditions.

1927 The Academy of Motion Picture Arts and Sciences hosts first awards ceremony.

1932 The Olympic Summer Games come to Exposition Park.

1955 Disneyland opens.

1965 Race riots in Watts rage for six days leaving 34 dead and 1,032 wounded.

1984 The Olympic Summer Games return to LA.

1992 Riots follow acquittal of four white police officers accused of beating black motorist Rodney King (► 12).

1993 Bush fires threaten Malibu and cause more than $200 million worth of damage.

1994 Northridge earthquake (6.8 on the Richter scale) kills 55 and does $30 billion damage.

1997 Opening of the $1 billion Getty Center arts and cultural complex.

1999 The $375 million Staples Center, home to the LA Lakers (basketball), Clippers (basketball) and Kings (ice hockey), opens Downtown.

2002 Frank Gehry's $27 million Disney Concert Hall opens across from the Music Center.

PEOPLE & EVENTS FROM HISTORY

The Los Angeles aqueduct

As LA boomed around the turn of the 20th century, the demand for water became a major issue. When water bureau superintendent William Mulholland suggested an aqueduct to transport melted snow from the Sierra Nevadas to feed the growing city, he was thought to be mad. However, Mulholland's aqueduct, all 223 miles and 142 tunnels of it, opened in 1913, and with a 105-mile extension into the Mono Basin, it still supplies the city. Roman Polanksi's *Chinatown* dramatises the early struggles in the area over water.

FATHER JUNÍPERO SERRA

Father Junípero Serra, a native of the Mediterranean island of Mallorca, was sent to Mexico to work as a missionary in 1749. In 1769, as Padre Presidente of the Spanish Franciscan missions in Baja (Lower) California, he accompanied the first governor of the Californias, Gaspar de Portolá, on a colonising expedition to San Diego. Here they founded the first of 21 California missions in a chain that would reach from San Diego north to Sonoma. San Gabriel Archangel, in the San Gabriel Valley, was the fourth, built with the help of Native Americans, later known as Gabrieleno Indians.

D W GRIFFITH

David Wark Griffith (1875–1948) is often regarded as film-making's greatest pioneer and innovator. He began his career in New York, then moved to Los Angeles where he made *The Birth of a Nation* (banned in some cities for its racist tone), followed in 1916 by the lavish *Intolerance* starring Lillian Gish. Working with cameraman Billy Bitzer, Griffith experimented with lighting and camera techniques. An early champion of the 'talkies', which he claimed would become 'the greatest artistic medium the world has ever known', Griffith was also responsible for toning down the melodramatic proclivities of contemporary stage actors, adapting their style for film.

THE 1992 LA RIOTS

When the videotaped 1991 beating of black motorist Rodney King by white LAPD officers failed to secure a single court conviction, racial tensions among LA's African-American community exploded in the country's most destructive episode of civil unrest this century. The first outbreak of violence came within hours of the not-guilty verdicts being delivered on 29 April 1992. Some 48 hours later, 52 people were dead, 2,400 injured, 1,600 businesses were closed for good, and property damage exceeded $1 billion.

D W Griffith directing
Battle of the Sexes

LOS ANGELES
how to organise your time

ITINERARIES

Los Angeles is so vast it makes sense to sightsee neighbourhood by neighbourhood, and a car is essential. Always check your map in advance and plot a route. Except Downtown, parking is easy and inexpensive.

ITINERARY ONE	HOLLYWOOD BOULEVARD TO HOLLYHOCK HOUSE
Morning	Start off outside Mann's Chinese Theater (► 55), then cross the street to the Hollywood Roosevelt Hotel (► 53) for a Hollywood history lesson. Stop by the Hollywood Entertainment Museum (► 53), Hollywood Guinness World of Records Museum (► 58) and Frederick's of Hollywood Lingerie Museum (► 52).
Lunch	Celebrity-spot at Musso & Frank grill (► 81), or picnic in Barnsdall Park at Hollyhock House (► 56). Late lunchers will find plenty of options on Melrose Avenue (► 70).
Afternoon	After a peek at Hollyhock House (► 56), undergoing restoration until 2003, take a detour via the Hollywood Memorial Park Cemetery (► 52) to Melrose Avenue (► 70).
ITINERARY TWO	SOUTH BAY (PALOS VERDES TO LONG BEACH)
Morning	Take the scenic route around the Palos Verdes headland (off the Pacific Coast Highway) via Lloyd Wright's Wayfarer's Chapel to San Pedro and the Los Angeles Maritime Museum (► 50). Kids might enjoy the free Cabrillo Aquarium (► 59) near by. The Banning Residence Museum (► 50) is en route to Long Beach and the *Queen Mary* (► 42). This is a good place to stop for lunch.
Lunch	Belmont Brewing Company (► 69).
Afternoon	The Long Beach Aquarium of the Pacific is a couple of minutes from Downtown. A 10-minute drive west, Rancho Los Alamitos, an 1806 landmark (► 43), is a delight.

ITINERARY THREE	**PASADENA**
Morning	The Huntington (➤ 46) does not open until noon on weekdays except in summer. However, Pasadena has much else to offer starting with the historic Mission San Gabriel Archangel (➤ 56). The Los Angeles State and County Arboretum (➤ 47) is a real treat, and the Descanso Gardens (➤ 57) are famous for camellias (Jan–Mar). Then head for Old Town Pasadena (➤ 70).
Lunch	There's plenty of choice for lunch in Pasadena, try the Market City Caffe (➤ 68) close to the Colorado Boulevard. Also the Gordon Biersch Brewery for alfresco eating (➤ 67) and The Raymond (➤ 62).
Afternoon	Visit the Huntington. Afterwards tour the stunning Gamble House (➤ 44; noon–3) or visit the Norton Simon Museum of Art (➤ 45; noon–6). Both are open afternoons only, Thursday to Sunday.
ITINERARY FOUR	**SANTA MONICA TO VENICE BEACH**
Morning	Hit the shops at Third Street Promenade and Santa Monica Place (➤ 70–71). Then head straight for Santa Monica Pier (➤ 24), where you can rent a bike for the day and coast down the beach bike path with detours off to shops and galleries on Main Street (between Hollister and Rose avenues), also home to architect Frank Gehry's Edgemar development ⊠ 2435 Main Street and the California Heritage Museum ⊠ 2612 Main Street
Lunch	Try the terrace at Rockenwagner (➤ 67), the patio of the World Café (➤ 68), or Venice's beachfront Sidewalk Café (➤ 68) for excellent people-watching.
Afternoon	Hit the beach after lunch. Or take a stroll around the canal district (➤ 26); stop by the landmark Frank Gehry building (➤ 55); and visit the Museum of Flying (➤ 58).

WALKS

AROUND DOWNTOWN: PERSHING SQUARE TO LITTLE TOKYO

Start off at Pershing Square with its purple bell-tower and multicoloured building block art installations, then cut through the sumptuously refurbished Biltmore Hotel to Grand Avenue. (The LA Conservancy's guided walking tours depart from the Biltmore on Saturdays ► 19). Take a turn around the Los Angeles Central Library, then, across 5th Street, climb the Bunker Hill Steps from the foot of the First Interstate World Center.

All aboard Angels Flight

Bunker Hill At the top of the city's glass-canyoned Financial District, the Wells Fargo History Museum is just across the road from the Museum of Contemporary Art (MOCA) and California Plaza. The Plaza is a good place to catch your breath and watch the dancing fountains before taking the Angels Flight funicular down to Grand Central Market. Walk through the market and cross Broadway to the Bradbury Building, near the corner with 3rd Street.

Coffee breaks There are several pavement café-coffee shops on the Bunker Hill Steps and at the Wells Fargo Center, plus the upscale cafeteria Patinette at the Museum of Contemporary Art (► 68).

Little Tokyo Shuttle bus DASH D operates from Spring Street (one block east on 3rd Street) to Union Station, passing within a block of Little Tokyo. You could also walk to 2nd Street (one block north), then east for Japanese Village Plaza.

Time for lunch Grand Central Market is a great place to eat cheaply; bakers, fruit sellers and deli stalls offer everything from tacos to Chinese noodles. Near Union Station is Philippe The Original (► 69) for sandwiches; on Olvera Street there are plenty of Mexican restaurants, including La Golondrina (► 66).

THE SIGHTS

- Biltmore Hotel (► 56)
- Los Angeles Central Library (► 56)
- Wells Fargo History Museum (► 36)
- MOCA (► 37)
- California Plaza (► 54)
- Angels Flight (► 54)
- Grand Central Market (► 38)
- Bradbury Building (► 39)
- Little Tokyo (► 40)

INFORMATION

Distance approx 1½ miles
Time 2–3 hours
Start point Pershing Square
🚇 M7
🚉 Pershing Square
🚌 DASH B, C, E
End point Little Tokyo
🚇 N7
🚌 DASH A, D

AROUND EL PUEBLO: UNION STATION TO CHINATOWN

Take time to explore inside the splendid Spanish Colonial-style Union Station building before walking up to the Old Plaza at the heart of El Pueblo de Los Angeles, the centre of the original settlement here. The tree-shaded plaza is flanked by historic buildings including the 1870 Pico House built by the last Mexican governor of California.

Olvera Street Stroll down this restored 19th-century street, tightly packed with the souvenir and craft stalls of a Mexican street market wedged between the historic brick façades. Here you will find lively pavement cafés and restaurants, appertising take-away taco stands and ice-cream and *churros* vendors do a swift trade. Stop off at the city's oldest dwelling, the Avila Adobe, which was founded in 1818 and has since been much enlarged. The Visitor Information Center, in the Sepulveda House, presents a short video showing a brief history of Los Angeles.

Avila Adobe, the city's oldest home

Chinatown Walk west a couple of blocks to Broadway, then north. Though no match for San Francisco's bustling Chinatown, the 900 block of Broadway boasts a handful of Asian-inspired bank buildings in the Bank of America, the East-West Bank, guarded by stone lion-dogs and the United Savings Bank on the corner of Sun-Yat-Sen Plaza, where there is a well-used wishing well. Around the plaza are restaurants, fortune tellers and shops selling a wide assortment of wares including incense, jade carvings, pottery and plum sauce.

THE SIGHTS

- Union Station (► 56)
- El Pueblo de Los Angeles Historic Park and Olvera Street (► 41)

INFORMATION

Distance approx 1¼ miles
Time 1½–2 hours
Start point Union Station
🚇 N6
🚉 Union Station
🚌 DASH B, D
End point Chinatown
🚇 N5
🚌 DASH B

17

EVENING STROLLS

Although LA is a car town, there are a couple of pedestrian-friendly enclaves where a post-prandial stroll is in order.

INFORMATION

Old Pasadena
Start point Between Arroyo Parkway and Delacey Avenue
✚ Off map, northeast
🚌 180, 181, 484

Olvera Street
Start point Old Plaza, El Pueblo de Los Angeles
✚ N6
🚉 Union Station
🚌 DASH B, D

Santa Monica
Start point Santa Monica Pier
✚ Off map, west
🚌 22, 322, 434, SM1, SM7, SM10

Westwood Village
Start point Westwood Boulevard (off Wilshire)
✚ Off map, west
🚌 20, 21, 22, 320, 322, SM1, SM2, SM3

The pier at Santa Monica is a favourite filming location

OLD PASADENA
This 20-block historic area, in one of LA's most affluent suburbs, also offers a wide choice of restaurants. Admire the handsome old brick buildings ornamented with decorative reliefs and wrought ironwork and do a bit of window-shopping (➤ 70).

OLVERA STREET
El Pueblo's Mexican street market continues well into the evening. Souvenir-hunting followed by people-watching over pre-dinner margaritas is a pastime here.

SANTA MONICA
Watch the sunset from the pier, then stroll to pedestrianised 3rd Street Promenade, edged by dozens of bars, cafés, shops and restaurants, which stay open late.

WESTWOOD VILLAGE
The magic triangle of Westwood Boulevard, Broxton and Weyburn avenues on the southern edge of the UCLA campus was actually designed to be pedestrian-friendly, a rare quality in LA. The architecture is 1920s Mediterranean Revival set in beautiful land-scaped grounds; inexpensive pavement cafés, coffee bars, restaurants with a wide range of cuisines and cinemas abound.

ORGANISED SIGHTSEEING

WALKING TOURS
Los Angeles Conservancy ☎ 213/623–2489
Excellent Saturday morning Downtown walking tours with options ranging from historic Broadway theatres to art-deco architecture.
JRT International – "Hiking in L.A." ☎ 818/501–1005
Scenic hiking tours with an educational angle in the Santa Monica Mountains.

BUS TOURS
Hollywood Fantasy Tours ☎ 323/469–8184 The classic star tours covering the famous and infamous sites and movie star homes of Hollywood and Beverly Hills.
Casablanca Tours ☎ 818/775–3982 Tour celebrity-haunts and houses by van or opt for the showbiz Hollywood Tour.

LIMOUSINE TOURS
Star Limousine Tours ☎ 310/829–1066 and **Ultra Tours** ☎ 310/274–1303 both offer tours of star homes and other Hollywood landmarks in stretch-limo luxury.

HELICOPTER TOURS
Heli U.S.A. Helicopters ☎ 310/641–9494 A great romantic night-time package with a spectacular flight over the city followed by dinner at DC3 (► 67). Also daytime flights.
Island Express Helicopters ☎ 310/510–2525 The fastest route to Catalina Island (► 20) from Long Beach and San Pedro, plus sightseeing, sunset, dinner and heli-golfing packages.

BOAT TRIPS
Gondola Getaway ☎ 562/433–9595 BYO champagne and the stripey-shirted gondolier will provide ice bucket, glasses and hors d'oeuvres to accompany a splendid Venetian-style gondola ride around the canals of Naples Island (Long Beach).
Shoreline Village Cruises ☎ 562/495–5884 Summer season harbour cruises and whale-watching expeditions (Jan–Apr) from Long Beach. Guaranteed whale sightings, or second trip for free.

NBC Studio tours
The only LA television studio to offer tours, NBC Studio (✉ 3000 W Alameda Avenue, Burbank ☎ 818/840–3537), invites visitors to take a look around its broadcasting complex. Check out the wardrobe and make-up departments, visit a special effects set and *The Tonight Show* set. Free tickets for that evening's show are available at the Studio's ticket counter. Get there early.

EXCURSIONS

INFORMATION

Topanga State Park

➕ Off map, west

✉ 20825 Entrada Road

☎ 310/455—2465

🕐 Daily 8–7 in summer; 8–5 in winter

🅿 Moderate parking fee

Solstice Canyon Park

➕ Off map, west

✉ 3800 Solstice Canyon Road

☎ 805/370—2301 (run by the National Park Service)

🕐 Daily 8–7 in summer; 8–5 in winter

🚌 434 to Corral Canyon Road

🅿 Moderate parking fee

Catalina Island

➕ Off map, southwest

🛳 Catalina Cruises (Long Beach)
   ☎ 800/228—2546
   Catalina Express (Long Beach and San Pedro)
   ☎ 800/464—4228

ℹ Catalina Island Visitors Bureau and Chamber of Commerce
   ☎ 310/510—1520

HIKING IN THE SANTA MONICA MOUNTAINS

One mile west of the Getty Museum, Topanga Canyon Boulevard climbs up from the Malibu seashore into the foothills of the Santa Monica Mountains. As it passes through the laid-back alternative community of Topanga Canyon, bear right on Entrada Road, signposted for Topanga State Park. Trails criss-cross the 9,000-acre chaparral reserve, winding through oak and sumac woodlands and across rolling pastures with views of the mountains and off to the ocean. Watch for red-tailed hawks wheeling overhead, California quail and even the occasional roadrunner.

Solstice Canyon Park, a former ranch off the Pacific Coast Highway just west of Malibu, is reckoned to have one of the finest walking trails in the mountains. There are two routes that form a convenient loop from the car park: the gentle 1½-mile Solstice International Trail, which is shady in summer, along an old ranch road to a waterfall grotto fed by Solstice Creek; and the connecting Rising Sun Trail, a 3-mile high chaparral hike with notable views.

CATALINA ISLAND

An idyllic island 26 miles off the coast, Catalina offers lovely beaches, great diving, a miraculously undeveloped interior and a herd of buffalo introduced when filming *The Vanishing American* in 1925. Take the Catalina Cruises ferry (1 hour 50 minutes), the catamaran (under an hour), or the Catalina Express hydrofoil (1 hour 10 minutes) to Avalon, and drop in at the Chamber of Commerce office on the pier for a map, and sightseeing, glass-bottomed boat, horse-riding and dive tour information (also hiking permits). Explore the pretty main town of Avalon, stopping off at the marvellous 1920s Casino and the Catalina Museum, then climb the hill to the Zane Grey Pueblo Hotel (► 85) for the harbour view. The cheap Catalina Safari Bus stops at beaches, trails, and campsites en route to Two Harbors resort village. An overnight stay is highly recommended; make a reservation well in advance.

MISSION SAN JUAN CAPISTRANO

The seventh of the California missions, San Juan Capistrano was founded in 1776. The picturesque ruins of the Stone Church are home to the famous swallows that are said to return here from Argentina for the summer every 19 March. Take time to wander in the pretty gardens, shaded by jacaranda trees and bright in season with camellias, roses, hibiscus and bougainvilleas. There is a blacksmith's shop and restored barrack buildings housing Spanish-era artefacts, plus the lovely painted adobe Serra Chapel. Beyond the mission, the town has Spanish-style buildings and several antiques shops on Camino Capistrano, plus a local history museum, located across the railway tracks.

INFORMATION

Mission San Juan Capistrano

- ✉ Ortega Highway
- ☎ 949/248–2040
- 🕐 Daily 8:30–5
- 🚆 Trains from Union Station
- 💲 Inexpensive

San Juan Capistrano

The two main driving routes south to San Juan are the fast, direct I-5/Santa Ana Freeway (about an hour from Downtown to the I-74 exit) and the Pacific Coast Highway, passing through Huntington, Newport and Laguna Beaches. It's slower, but it's spectacular seaside vistas, farther north especially, make it one of the most famous drives in the world.

J PAUL GETTY MUSEUM, MALIBU

Since 1997 the new Getty Center (► 25) has housed the bulk of the Getty collections while the Malibu site is renovated before reopening in 2002 as a showcase for the stunning Getty antiquities. The superb displays of Greek and Roman art will be housed in the reconstruction of a Roman villa based on the Villa dei Papyri, which was destroyed by the eruption of Mount Vesuvius in AD 79.

J Paul Getty Museum

- ✚ Off map, west
- ✉ 17985 Pacific Coast Highway
- ☎ Information: 310/458–2003

WHAT'S ON

For up-to-date details and more information on local happenings check with the Los Angeles Convention and Visitor Bureau Events Hotline ☎ 213/689–8822. The Calendar section of Sunday's *Los Angeles Times* provides a weekly guide, as does the free *LA Weekly*.

January	*Rose Parade*: Pasadena's New Year's Day spectacular features marching bands and extravagant floats, along with the Rose Bowl football game.
February	*Chinese New Year*: A Golden Dragon Parade winds its way through Chinatown.
March	*Academy Awards*: Celebrities gather Downtown.
May	*Cinco de Mayo*: Mexicans celebrate Mexico's independence from France (1867) with feasting, music and dance. Olvera Street is a good place to join in the fun.
June	*Gay and Lesbian Pride Celebration*: Massive weekend event held around West Hollywood Park. Also in June, the Annual Mariachi-USA Festival at the Hollywood Bowl.
July–August	*Nisei Week*: Dance and martial arts demonstrations, crafts and food stalls as Little Tokyo celebrates Japanese-American cultural heritage.
July–September	*Hollywood Bowl Summer Festival*: Evening open-air concerts at the home of the LA Philharmonic, with a broad-ranging programme – classical music, jazz and pops.
October	*AFI Film Festival*: The American Film Institute descends on LA for a week-long independent and foreign film binge.
November	*Dia de los Muertos*: Folklorico musicians, puppet shows, Mexican music and crafts on Olvera Street for the Day of the Dead. *Doo Dah Parade*: Pasadena's irreverent Rose Parade spoof.
December	*Hollywood Christmas Parade*: Major floats, marching bands, classic cars, celebrity guests.

LOS ANGELES'
top 25 sights

The sights are shown on the maps on the inside front cover and inside back cover, numbered **1–25** *from west to east across the city*

1

SANTA MONICA & MALIBU

INFORMATION

Inside front cover
Santa Monica Visitor Center
✉ ♪ 400 Ocean Avenue (between Santa Monica Boulevard and Colorado Avenue)
☎ 310/393–7593
🕐 Daily 10–4 (until 5 in summer)
🍴 Many restaurants, bars and cafés
🚌 SM1, SM2, 4, 20, 33, 304
♿ Good to nonexistent depending on location
↔ J Paul Getty Museum (► 21)
Will Rogers State Historic Park (► 57)
Museum of Flying (► 58)
Bergamot Station (► 74)
❓ Walking tours of Santa Monica murals:
☎ 310/822–9560

Malibu surfing reports:
310/457–9701

Tanned bodies playing volleyball, the crowded bike path, plus great shopping and drinking on the bustling promenade and environs, draw crowds to this enduringly popular stretch of coast.

Pier pressure Santa Monica's landmark 1909 pier still exudes that old-fashioned amusement-park aura which evokes a fuzzy nostalgia in adults and requests for money from attendant offspring. Along the weathered wooden boardwalk, Pacific Park's (► 58) giant Ferris wheel and roller-coaster loom above the restored 1922 carousel operated by Paul Newman in *The Sting*. Down at beach level, the UCLA Ocean Discovery Center presents marine exhibits, aquariums and touch tanks. You can also rent a bike or in-line skates to swoop along the 26-mile concrete beach path.

Beyond the beach Santa Monica's inland entertainment hub is Third Street Promenade, four pedestrianised blocks of shops, cafés and cinemas. For a more esoteric experience, check out Main Street (between Hollister and Rose avenues), with its trendy restaurants and art galleries and the California Heritage Museum at Ocean Park (► 15).

Continuing along the coast Quieter and more remote than Santa Monica, its southern neighbour, the lovely enclave of Mailibu, lures daytime visitors with its 27 miles of sprawling beaches and canyons; this is where people come for romantic restaurant hideaways. Despite its drawbacks – traffic, brush fires and mud slides – plenty of Hollywood luminaries hang their hats here. The real draw, though, isn't celeb sightings or dining but the surfing. Check out the waves and call for a surf report.

THE GETTY CENTER

Carved into the foothills of West LA's Santa Monica Mountains, Richard Meier's magnificent Getty Center impresses visitors with its eye-catching landscape and breathtaking views of the city.

The background Oil billionaire J Paul Getty began collecting in the 1930s and a passion for Greek and Roman antiquities inspired the J Paul Getty Museum at Malibu (▶ 21). After his death in 1976 and his $700 million bequest, the size of its collections swelled. Opened in 1997, the $1 billion Getty Center houses this trove of 13th- to 19th-century Western art as well as the J Paul Getty Trust's arts education, research and funding programmes.

Treasure Part fortress, part piazza, and focus of the 24-acre complex, the stunning inside-out architecture is a triumph. Five honey-coloured pavilions flank the central courtyard. The first four display the collections in chronological order; decorative arts and sculpture are on the ground floor and paintings from the corresponding period on the upper level; the fifth pavilion houses special exhibitions.

Art First you will see medieval and Renaissance works, from the Ludwig illuminated manuscripts to the works of Fra Angelico. Next, stroll by the Old Masters – works by Brueghel, Rembrandt, Rubens and Van Dyck. There are also splendid English portraits, grand galleries of 18th-century French decorative arts and memorable 19th-century images, from Civil War photographs to Van Gogh's *Irises*. Step outside to the outdoor café or to explore the gardens, whose elegant geometric plantings have a distinctly Zen feel. The Getty's one drawback is its steady crowds.

HIGHLIGHTS

- Ludwig Manuscripts
- Old Master Gallery
- French decorative arts
- *Irises*, Van Gogh

INFORMATION

- ✚ Inside front cover
- ✉ 1200 Getty Center Drive, off I–405/San Diego Freeway
- ☎ 310/440–7300
- 🕐 Tue–Wed 11–7; Thu–Fri 11–9; Sat–Sun 10–6. Closed public hols

Top: Coronation of the Virgin, *da Fabriano. Above:* Bacchante, *ter Brugghen*

- 🍴 Restaurant (reservations essential) and cafés
- 🚌 561, SM14. Ask driver for free admission pass
- ♿ Excellent
- 💲 Museum free. Parking moderate (reservations essential)
- ❓ Audioguides, talks, concerts

25

3

VENICE BEACH

HIGHLIGHTS

- Muscle Beach
- Ocean Front Walk
- Venice Canal Walkway (access from S Venice Boulevard)
- Venice Boardwalk
- Venice Pier
- Numerous art galleries

INFORMATION

✚ Inside front cover
Santa Monica Visitor Center
✉ 1400 Ocean Avenue (between Santa Monica Boulevard and Colorado Avenue), Santa Monica

☎ 310/393–7593
🕐 Daily 10–4 (until 5 in summer)
🍴 Restaurants, bars and cafés
🚌 SM1, 4, 33
♿ Good to nonexistent depending on location
↔ Frank Gehry Building on Main Street (➤ 55)

Venice Area Chamber of Commerce
✉ Post Office Box 202, Venice, Cali 90294
☎ 310/396–7016

❓ Free workshops and readings at the Beyond Baroque Literary Arts Center and Bookshop ✉ City Hall ☎ 310/822–3006

Best known for its beachfront boardwalk, bohemian Venice Beach is also home to a flourishing artists' community, lovely outdoor dining, and sadly, a gang presence. People–watching is the number one pastime, but shopping comes a close second.

The action Where Main crosses Rose Street, Joseph Borofsky's *Ballerina Clown* figure greets visitors to Venice. It is an appropriate icon for this entertaining beach community, a throwback to the psychedelic Sixties combined with the narcissism of Muscle Beach. Ocean Front Walk is where it all hangs out, a non-stop parade of scantily clad humanity, shiny body-builders, funky street performers, tourists and stalls.

Italian dream Developer Abbot Kinney created this American snapshot of Venice, Italy, in the early 1900s as a tribute to its European counterpart, and the Venice Canal Walkway, just inland from Ocean Front Walk, explores the quiet, canal-lined residential neighbourhood that gave the area its name. Venice, California, has earned itself both starring roles and bit parts in various films – as the seedy backdrop in Orson Welles' *Touch of Evil*, for example, and as the fictious Rydell High in the 1970s musical *Grease*.

Join the buzz Energetic visitors should consider renting a bike or a pair of rollerblades to join the masses on Ocean Front Walk. Afterwards, take a stroll down Main Street, the artery that connects Santa Monica and Venice, and check out the shops, buildings and art galleries. Crowds flock to the area, but do exercise caution at night.

UCLA HAMMER MUSEUM

Roundly criticised for its architecture, the lack of 'importance' of its collections, even for its existence, the Hammer is not a big favourite with the neighbourhood cultural panjandrums. However, there are several worthwhile small-scale treasures here.

Hammer and tongs Much of the highbrow carping about the Hammer is probably based on the general dislike of Armand Hammer himself. The immensely rich and acquisitive man, an oil millionaire many times over, originally promised his art collections to a number of local institutions. When he decided to build his own museum instead, the news was greeted with dismay.

Minor miracles Modest in size, the Hammer is a respite from more overwhelming local museums. Its collection is composed mainly of Impressionist and Post-Impressionist works by painters such as Monet, Pissarro, and Mary Cassatt; complementary works from UCLA's own collections are also shown here.

Changing exhibitions Selections from the 19th-century Daumier and His Contemporaries Collection, featuring paintings, sculpture and lithographs by the leading French satirist of the age, are shown in rotation. The museum is also a showcase for the UCLA Grunwald Center for the Graphic Arts. This collection comprising more than 35,000 prints, drawings, photographs and book illustrations, containing works by such luminaries as Dürer, Cézanne, Matisse and Jasper Johns, is displayed in other themed exhibitions. Check out the museum's temporary programme.

HIGHLIGHTS

- *Beach at Trouville*, Boudin
- *Dans l'Omnibus*, Vuillard
- Grunwald Center exhibitions
- *Hospital at Saint-Rémy*, Van Gogh
- *Mme Hessel at the Seashore*, Vuillard
- *The Sower*, Van Gogh
- *Street Scene*, Bonnard

INFORMATION

- ✚ Inside front cover
- ✉ 10899 Wilshire Boulevard, Westwood
- ☎ 310/443–7000
- 🕐 Tue–Sat 11–7 (Thu 11–9); Sun 11–5
- 🍴 Courtyard café
- 🚌 20, 21, 22, 320
- ♿ Very good
- 💲 Moderate
- ↔ Westwood Village (➤ 18 and 70)
  UCLA's Franklin D Murphy Sculpture Garden (➤ 59)

Above: Two Actors, Honoré Daumier
Right: bust of Armand Hammer

5

BEVERLY HILLS

Love it or loathe it, you can't say you've 'done Los Angeles' until you've seen Beverly Hills. The city's most recognisable zip code (90210) is also LA's most visited neighbourhood, receiving over 14 million visitors a year.

A star is born In a classic rags-to-riches story, the countrified suburb of Beverly Hills, west of Hollywood, was plucked from obscurity by the movies – Douglas Fairbanks Jr to be exact, who set up home here in 1919, followed by Charlie Chaplin, Gloria Swanson and Rudolph Valentino.

The Golden Triangle Today, Beverly Hills remains ostentatiously star-studded, a monument to conspicuous consumption. For black-belt window shopping, there's the Golden Triangle, bounded by Crescent Drive and Wilshire and Santa Monica boulevards and bisected by world-famous Rodeo Drive, a showpiece three-block strip of designer emporiums. At the Wilshire Boulevard end, the $200-million self-proclaimed 'European-style' Via Rodeo fashion retail complex features real cobblestones, a miniaturised version of Rome's Spanish Steps, and the busiest branch of jewellers Tiffany & Co. outside Manhattan.

Seeing the sights A historical Beverly Hills walking tour map is available from the Visitors Bureau. The walk takes about two hours and covers such local sights as the imposing City Hall, Beverly Gardens and the wonderful Gaudí-like O'Neill House at No. 507 N Rodeo Drive (go down the alley to admire the swirling stucco and mosaic inlay of the guest house). If you want to see movie moguls at play, try the Polo Lounge at the flamingo-pink Beverly Hills Hotel (▶ 84).

PETERSEN AUTOMOTIVE MUSEUM

Displaying more than requisite classic cars, the Peterson Automotive Museum traces the automobile's evolution, along with celebrity cruisers and the physics behind driving.

Driving through history The largest museum of its kind in the US, the Petersen explores automotive history and culture from early jalopies to the sleek dream machines of the Testa Rossa zone. The ground-floor 'Streetscape', a series of dioramas and displays designed to illustrate the effects of motoring on people's lives, kicks off with a 1911 American Underslung touring car and continues via a classic Laurel and Hardy scene involving a Ford Model T, to a 1929 gas station, and a glossy 1930s new car showroom complete with cigar-chomping buyer. 'L.A. Autotude' salutes the automobile as fashion accessory with a selection of bizarre cars, and there are tributes to the 1950s, as well as the 1960s, and displays of vehicles of the future.

Capital of customising On the second floor, the galleries are always changing, displaying stars' cars in the Hollywood Gallery; LA hot rods from California's capital of customising and the absorbing Otis Chandler Motorcycle Gallery.

Top: diorama of 1911 touring car. Right: car showroom, 1930s

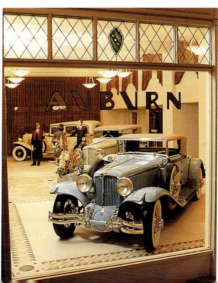

7

LA COUNTY MUSEUM OF ART

HIGHLIGHTS

- Drawings and pastels, Degas
- Edo scrolls and netsuke, Japanese Pavilion
- Moscow Avant-Garde School paintings and drawings (Kandinsky and Rodchenko)
- *Jazz Facsimile*, Matisse
- *La Pipe*, Magritte
- Persian illuminated manuscripts
- *Untitled*, Rothko
- *Waterlilies*, Monet

INFORMATION

- ✚ Inside front cover
- ✉ 5905 Wilshire Boulevard, Midtown
- ☎ 323/857–6000
- 🕐 Mon, Tue, Thu noon–8; Fri noon–9; Sat–Sun 11–8. Closed Thanksgiving, Christmas
- 🍴 Plaza Café
- 🚌 20, 21, 22, 217, 320, 322
- ♿ Very good
- 💲 Moderate
- ↔ Petersen Automotive Museum (► 29) George C Page Museum of La Brea (► 50) Farmer's Market (► 71)

One of the finest, most broad-ranging art museums in the United States, LACMA also draws kudos for alfresco jazz concerts in the courtyard plaza on Friday evenings and Sunday afternoons.

The collections The majority of the museum's permanent collections are housed in the Ahmanson Building. Here magnificent examples of ancient Asian, Egyptian and pre Columbian art, medieval and Renaissance paintings, works by 17th-century Dutch landscape specialists and 18th-century French Romantics have been gathered together with a feast of Impressionist, Fauvist, Cubist and Surrealist art. There is a dazzling array of British silver, diverse examples of European and American decorative arts, plus costumes and textiles, jewel-like Persian manuscripts and Ottoman ceramics. The museum boasts world-class collections of 20th-century German and German Expressionist art, and the Bruce Goff Japanese Pavilion is a work of art in itself.

Exhibitions and sculpture gardens In addition to housing selections from the permanent collections, the Anderson and Hammer Buildings offer acres of special exhibition space, and LACMA is a great place to catch top-flight visiting exhibitions. The buildings are flanked by sculpture gardens with works by Rodin, Bourdelle, Calder and Alice Aycock.

Make a plan The museum complex is spread over five buildings. Its collections are so vast and varied that there is far too much to be seen comfortably in a single visit, so it is advisable to plot a route around personal favourites with the aid of a layout plan (constantly changing) from the information booth.

Portrait of an Artist (Pool with Two Figures), *David Hockney*

HOLLYWOOD BOULEVARD

Though Hollywood Boulevard's 1930s and 1940s heyday is a distant memory, movie buffs can still get a kick out of inspecting Trigger's hoofprints outside Mann's Chinese Theater.

Facelift After almost 50 years of decay and decline, Tinseltown's most evocative address is undergoing a major facelift. One of the first things to be buffed up along the boulevard has been the Hollywood Walk of Fame. Stretching between Gower Street and La Brea Avenue, with an annexe on Vine, almost 2,000 bronze stars set in the pavement honour celebrities in film, television, theatre and radio. The select few invited to place their hands, feet, hooves, or (in the case of Betty Grable) legs in the concrete courtyard of Mann's Chinese Theater (▶ 55) include Marilyn Monroe, Sylvester Stallone and Cary Grant. Here, booths sell self-guided Hollywood star site maps; Tourlands's hearse expeditions (▶ 53) are the best insider guide to Hollywood deviancy and shenanigans.

Hollywood history Sid Grauman, who built the Chinese Theater, was also one of the founding partners in the Hollywood Roosevelt Hotel (▶ 53) across the street. A couple of Michelle Pfeiffer's nightclub scenes from *The Fabulous Baker Boys* were filmed here. The Hollywood Enertainment Museum (▶ 53) is an interesting stop nearby; an assortment of celebrity figures can be found in the Hollywood Wax Museum at 6767 Hollywood Boulevard, while kids might enjoy the Hollywood Guinness World of Records Museum (▶ 58).

INFORMATION

➕ E1

Visitors Information Center

✉ Janes House, 6541 Hollywood Boulevard, Hollywood

☎ 213/689–8822 (events hotline)

🕐 Mon–Sat 9–5

🚍 1, 217

🎟 Free

↔ Hollyhock House (▶ 56) Frederick's of Hollywood Lingerie Museum (▶ 52) Hollywood Memorial Park Cemetery (▶ 52) Capitol Records Tower (▶ 54)

Above: Mann's Chinese Theater. Below: the famous hand- and footprints outside it

UNIVERSAL STUDIOS

INFORMATION

- ✚ Inside front cover
- ✉ Universal City Drive (off I–101/Hollywood Freeway)
- ☎ 818/622–3801
- ◷ Summer: daily 8AM–10PM (box office 7–5). Winter: daily 9–7 (box office 8:30–4). Closed Thanksgiving, Christmas
- 🍴 Wide range of dining and fast-food options
- 🚌 420, 424, 425, 522
- ♿ Good
- 💵 Very expensive (tickets include admission to rides, shows and attractions); children under 3 free. Parking: moderate
- ↔ Griffith Park (➤ 33)
- ❓ Regularly scheduled Spanish- and Japanese-language tram tours. French-language tours can be booked ahead

The world's biggest and busiest motion picture and television studio-cum-theme park is a great family day out. The admission charge is steep, but the classic Backlot Tram Tour and more recent **Jurassic Park** *are alone worth your hard-earned dollars.*

Back to the beginning Universal Studios' founder Carl Laemmle moved his movie studio facility to the Hollywood Hills in 1915 and inaugurated Universal Studios tours during the silent movie era. The arrival of the talkies put an end to live audiences until 1964, when trolley tours began; trolleys are still used to circle the 415-acre backlot.

Orientation To get the most out of your day, pick up a copy of the daily schedule at the entrance; it lists the various shows and attractions. At the top of everyone's list is the Backlot Tour – the latest incarnation of the tour that started it all – which includes close encounters with old banana breath himself in *Kongfrontation*, Jaws snapping his way around Amity Harbor, the ground-trembling *Earthquake: The Big One*, and classic locations from the *Psycho* house to the Little Europe Streetscape. Trolley tours depart from the Upper Lot, which is also home to the thrilling *Back to the Future* simulator ride and half-a-dozen great shows and revues including the distinctly gunky and slimy kid's TV favourite, *Totally Nickelodeon*.

Take a ride A quarter-mile escalator links the Upper Lot to the Lower Lot, the heart of the working studio complex. Here Universal's $100 million *Jurassic Park – The Ride* adventure visits a land of five-storey dinosaurs built with the help of aerospace scientists. There are red hot special effects at the *Backdraft* presentation, explanations of behind-the-scenes technology at *The World of Cinemagic*, and a cute cycle ride with *E.T.*

10

GRIFFITH PARK

A vast open-air playground straddling the Hollywood hills, Griffith Park offers a raft of sights and activities, the Autry Museum (➤ 35), and, from its landmark copper-domed Observatory, the best view of the Hollywood sign.

A handsome bequest The largest municipal park in the United States, Griffith Park lies in the foothills of the Santa Monica Mountains. The original 3,015-acre site was given to the city in 1896 by Col Griffith Jenkins Griffith, who also left a trust with sufficient funds to build the amphitheatre-style Greek Theater in 1930, a favourite outdoor concert venue, and the Griffith Observatory, which overlooks the city and houses an astronomy museum. There are daily planetarium and laserium shows, and on clear evenings you can see the heavens through a giant Zeiss telescope.

Around the park The huge park offers a tremendous variety of scenery. You can walk the cool, leafy Ferndell trail or reach the rugged high chaparral by a network of trails and easy-to-follow fire roads (maps from the Ranger Station). In the southeast corner of the park, near the Los Feliz exit, there are miniature train rides and children's pony rides. The antique merry-go-round, near the single, centrally located Ranger Station, is beloved of small children, and there are picnic areas, 28 tennis courts and four golf courses (➤ 83) with plenty of parking nearby. Further north, the Los Angeles Zoo showcases 1,200 animals on 77 landscaped acres. Northwest, off Zoo Drive, the Los Angeles Equestrian Center rents out American quarter horses. The park's one Ranger Station can also supply a list of stables in the park area, including Sunset Ranch, which offers visitors escorted moonlight rides.

DID YOU KNOW?

- Size: 4,107 acres
- Elevation: between 384 and 1,625 feet above sea level
- The Observatory starred in the 1955 movie *Rebel Without a Cause*
- Santana, Johnny Mathis and other acts selling over 100,000 tickets are commemorated in the Greek Theater's Wall of Fame

INFORMATION

- ✚ Inside front cover
- ✉ Off I–5/Golden State Freeway and 134/Ventura Freeway in the north
- ☎ Ranger Station: 323/913–4688. Griffith Park Observatory: 323/664–1191. Laserium Concerts 818/997–3624. Los Angeles Equestrian Center: 818/840–9063. Los Angeles Zoo: 323/666–4650
- ◷ Daily 6–10 (trails and mountain roads close at sunset). Merry-Go-Round: weekends 11–5; daily in summer. Miniature train rides: daily 10–4:30. Pony rides: Tue–Sun 10–5
- 🍴 Refreshment stands
- 🚌 96
- ♿ Good to nonexistent
- 💲 Park entry and observatory: free. Fees for some other attractions and shows
- ↔ Autry Museum of Western Heritage (➤ 35)

Natural History Museum

DID YOU KNOW?

- The total weight of a swarm of African locusts: 300 million pounds (1,500 tons)
- The Jurassic fish with teeth longer than a great white shark: *Xiphactonus audax*
- The world's deepest natural diver: Emperor penguin (840 feet)
- World's fastest diver: peregrine falcon (180mph)
- The famous US prison named for a bird: Alcatraz (Spanish for pelican)
- The two biggest bird stars of jungle movie soundtracks: the Australian kookaburra and Indian blue peafowl

INFORMATION

- J11
- 900 Exposition Boulevard
- 213/263–3466
- Daily 10–5. Closed Thanksgiving, Christmas, New Year's Day
- Cafeteria
- 40, 42, 81; DASH C/Expo Park
- Very good
- Moderate
- Exposition Park Rose Garden (► 57)

Enjoy a collection that dates back 400 million years at this imaginatively designed natural history museum, which also houses engaging exhibits on California's and LA's more recent past.

The broad picture The museum's home is a handsome Spanish Renaissance Revival affair on the north side of Exposition Park. Its collections cover an enormous range of topics. In addition to the natural history exhibits there are superb Mesoamerican artefacts including gold jewellery and pottery from the Maya, Inca and Aztec cultures; an excellent Native American Indian section with a re-created pueblo, intricate Plains Indian beadwork and Navajo textiles; and California and American history galleries.

Natural wonders Much to the delight of *Jurassic Park* fans, the County Museum is big on fossils and dinosaurs. This is the place to ogle a *Sauropod*, a pin-headed 72-foot long giant and one of the largest dinosaurs ever discovered. It probably weighed around 30–40 tons, dwarfing *Tyrannosaurus rex* (a mere 50 feet long and 6–7 tons). *Carnotaurus*, the meat-eating monster first discovered in Patagonia in 1984, also puts in an appearance, as does the rhino-like *Brontops*, or 'Thunderbeast'. The giant dioramas of African and North American mammals are terrific; and, on the geological front, there is a glittering Hall of Gems and Minerals. Do not miss the brilliant Discovery Zone. Children love the imaginative touchy-feely games and toys, fossil rubbings and other hands-on diversions. On the mezzanine level, the Insect Zoo offers a suitably creepy-crawly collection of slumbering scorpions, huge hissing cockroaches from Madagascar, pink-toed tarantulas and nauseating assassin bugs.

12

AUTRY MUSEUM OF WESTERN HERITAGE

It's hard to walk away from this spirited and entertaining celebration of all things Western without coveting a Stetson or a bandanna. The seven galleries provide a riveting insight into American Western history and heritage.

The singing cowboy Housed in a California Mission-style complex, the museum is named for Gene Autry, singing cowboy of Hollywood Westerns and early TV fame. The Autry Foundation was a prime mover in the establishment of the museum, which tells the story of the West through its magnificent collections of Western art and artefacts – over 40,000 individual pieces.

Winning the West The wagon-train era exhibit is enlivened by recorded extracts from pioneer diaries and Indian artefacts, and real gold nuggets add a frisson of authenticity to tales of the California Gold Rush. The Spirit of the Community gallery explores European, Mexican and Chinese migration in the Old West with lifestyle displays illustrating customs, costumes and crafts. The Cowboy Gallery, full of all sorts of cowboy accoutrements, introduces famous gunslingers – and the guns they slung – plus the Spanish *vaqueros* who were herding cattle on horseback for 300 years before Mexican *charros*, the cowboys of popular imagery. Kids dress up in boots and spurs in the Children's Discovery Gallery. Upstairs, the interesting Spirit of Imagination Gallery takes an intelligent look at Western culture as portrayed on screen.

HIGHLIGHTS

- Colt Firearms Collection
- Early art from the West
- Frederick Remington's bronze statues
- Indian beadwork and folk crafts
- Listening to recorded readings from pioneer diaries
- Trails West environmental display
- Western film and television memorabilia

INFORMATION

- 🔲 Inside front cover
- ✉ 4700 Western Heritage Way, Griffith Park (junction of I–5/Golden State Freeway and 134/Ventura Freeway)
- ☎ 323/667–2000
- 🕐 Tue–Sun 10–5; Thu until 8. Closed Thanksgiving, Christmas
- 🍴 Golden Spur Café
- ▣ 96
- ♿ Excellent
- 🎨 Moderate
- ↔ Universal Studios (► 32) Griffith Park (► 33)
- ❓ Frequent special exhibitions

13

WELLS FARGO HISTORY MUSEUM

DID YOU KNOW?

- Average speed of a Concord Stagecoach: 5mph
- Number of horses: 6 (changed every 12 miles)
- Duration of journey from Omaha to Sacramento: 15 days
- Cost: $300
- Baggage limit: 25lb per person
- Pony Express: operational April 1860 to October 1861
- Original route (duration): St Joseph, MO, to Sacramento, CA (1,966 miles in 10–12 days)
- Total mail carried: 35,000 letters

INFORMATION

- M7
- 333 S Grand Avenue
- 213/253–7166
- Mon–Fri 9–5
- DASH B
- Good
- Free
- Museum of Contemporary Art (➤ 37)
  Grand Central Market (➤ 38)
  California Plaza (➤ 54)
  Biltmore Hotel (➤ 56)
  Los Angeles Central Library (➤ 56)

An Old West legend right up there with the Colt Six-Shooter, Wyatt Earp and Buffalo Bill Cody, Wells Fargo celebrates the company's rip-roaring early history with tales of the Forty-Niners, the Pony Express and Concord Stagecoaches.

Expanding west By 1852, when Henry Wells and William G Fargo set up their Western banking and express service in San Francisco, the California Gold Rush was in full swing. The new venture swiftly established a reputation for buying, selling and transporting gold and valuables. In the early 1860s, Wells, Fargo & Co took over the western leg of the famed Pony Express. They operated a stagecoach service from the 1860s, and were among the first to take to the rails when the transcontinental railroad was completed in 1869.

'Cradle on Wheels' Centre stage in the museum goes to an original Concord Stagecoach, named for its birthplace in Concord, Mass. Though Mark Twain romantically described it as an 'imposing cradle on wheels', the reality of a stagecoach journey was far from relaxing. Up to 18 passengers, including the driver and guard, could be squeezed into the nine-seat leather upholstered interior and on to the open-air upper deck. Stops were infrequent, the food barely edible and, aside from the constant jolting, dust and discomfort, perils of the road included robbery and frequent accidents. Among the other artefacts on display, there is no missing the plum-sized gold nugget found in California's Feather River, near Challenge, in 1975. This lucky find weighed in at 26.4oz. Another eye-catcher is a 7,500lb, 19th-century safe handpainted with tranquil pastoral scenes and flowers, supposed to allay customers' concerns.

14

MUSEUM OF CONTEMPORARY ART

A single museum with two addresses a mile apart, MOCA has a growing catalogue of post-1940 artworks that constitutes one of the most important contemporary art collections in the United States.

Downtown All blonde wood and vast white spaces, MOCA's Downtown galleries, designed by Japanese architect Arata Isozaki, present a frequently changing programme of works drawn from the extensive permanent collection and touring exhibitions. The busy calendar also introduces newly commissioned projects and works by established and emerging artists in a broad variety of media.

Across town While Isozaki's museum was under construction, MOCA transformed a spacious warehouse in Little Tokyo into gallery space, now known as the Geffen Contemporary at MOCA. The vast industrial space, with its ramps and girders, is ideal for big installation pieces. Smaller works occupy a maze of galleries overlooked from a mezzanine level. In an interesting display designed to provide a loose comparative time-frame for contemporary art, a series of four 'context rooms' notes major historical, political and artistic developments since the 1940s.

HIGHLIGHTS

Works by:
- De Kooning
- Giacometti
- Mondrian
- Pollock
- Oldenburg
- Hockney

INFORMATION

MOCA
- ✛ M7
- ✉ 250 S Grand Avenue
- ☎ 213/626–6222
- ◷ Tue–Sun 11–5 (Thu until 8). Closed Thanksgiving, Christmas, New Year's Day
- 🍴 Patinette at MOCA (➤ 68)
- 🚌 DASH B
- ♿ Good
- 💲 Moderate (includes both buildings); free on Thu after 5
- ↔ Wells Fargo History Museum (➤ 36)
  California Plaza (➤ 54)
  Biltmore Hotel (➤ 56)
  Los Angeles Central Library (➤ 56)
- ❓ Regularly scheduled art talks programme, free with museum admission

Geffen Contemporary
- ✛ N7
- ✉ 152 N Central Avenue
- 🚌 DASH A
- ↔ Little Tokyo (➤ 40)
  Japanese American National Museum (➤ 50)

15

GRAND CENTRAL MARKET

DID YOU KNOW?

- *Mole*: a spicy Oaxacan sauce usually served over meat and prepared with chillies and chocolate
- *Chipotle*: smoked jalapeño pepper with a sweet taste
- *Churros*: deep-fried pastry
- *Criadillas*: bull's testicles
- *Gorditas*: fried corn and potato pockets filled with meat and beans
- *Tamales*: corn dough parcels filled with chicken or meat, or with almonds and raisins

INFORMATION

- M7
- 317 S Broadway
- 213/624–2378
- Mon–Sat 9–6; Sun 10–5
- Several Mexican fast-food take-away stalls, Chinese noodle café and a juice bar
- Civic Center
- DASH D
- Angels Flight
- None
- Free
- Wells Fargo History Museum (► 36)
  Museum of Contemporary Art (► 37)
  Bradbury Building (► 39)
  California Plaza (► 54)
  Biltmore Hotel (► 56)

Sawdust coats the floor and butchers' knives chop-chop and thud away on a dozen counters, just as they have for the last 80-plus years at this bustling, thriving Downtown LA landmark.

Downtown's historic larder LA's largest and oldest food market, a maze of closely packed stalls, first opened its doors in 1917, and the hangar like building, with entrances on both Broadway and Hill Street, has been feeding the Downtown district ever since. In those days, Broadway was LA's poshest thoroughfare, while today it is the heart of the city's crowded Hispanic shopping district. The market steps up several gears from busy to seething on Saturdays when the noise and the bustle is unbelievable.

Capsicums and cacti For anyone who loves food or markets, Grand Central is a real find. A fantastic feast for the eyes, it is also a great place to grab picnic food or stop for a snack. Capsicums, avocados and big beefy tomatoes are stacked into glossy piles alongside stalks of celery, potatoes in myriad hues, huge bunches of bananas, and pyramids of oranges, lemons and apples. Among the less familiar offerings are prickly pears, cactus leaves and dozens of different types of fresh and dried chillies available in varying degrees of ferocity. Meanwhile, the Mexican butchers display bits of beasts one would rather not even think about – vegetarians will want to avoid this area. There are more than 50 stalls in all, including fish merchants and bakers, delicatessens selling cheese and cold meats, spice merchants, dried fruit and nut sellers and the Chinese herbal medicine man. Take-away food stalls do a roaring trade in Mexican snacks, and there are quick-bite stops with tables and chairs near the Hill Street exit.

16

BRADBURY BUILDING

Inspired by a ouija–board and a science fiction novel, a young, unknown architect, George Wyman, took on a bold challenge and created the Bradbury, one of LA's hidden treasures.

A millionaire's monument In 1892 elderly and ailing mining millionaire Lewis Bradbury turned down the plans of respected local architect Sumner Hunt for a splendid five-storey building he wished to construct as a monument to his achievements. Instead, for no explicable reason, he invited an obscure architect's draftsman, 32-year-old George Wyman, to submit designs. Wyman initially refused, but one evening as he sat at a ouija-board with his wife, they received a message from his dead brother, which read 'Take the Bradbury building. It will make you famous'. Spurred on by this occult communication, and inspired by Edward Bellamy's 1887 science fiction novel *Looking Backward*, which actually looked forward to life in a Utopian society in the year 2000, Wyman created a dazzling futuristic building that ranks among the marvels of the age.

From fiction to fact The Italianate façade of the Bradbury, just across the street from the Grand Central Market, is attractive but unexceptional. However, the soaring, light-filled atrium is amazing. Light pours down through the narrow well, drawing the eye immediately upward and dramatising the sensation of height. Against a backdrop of golden-yellow Mexican tiles, pink glazed brick and polished oak, intricate, black wrought-iron railings edge the balconies and flights of marble steps climb five storeys to the roof. Wyman was never to design another significant building. Unfortunately Lewis Bradbury died just before his monument was opened in 1893.

DID YOU KNOW?

- Wyman imported Belgian marble for the staircases, and the French wrought-iron decorations were displayed at the 1893 Chicago World Fair before being installed
- The building cost Bradbury $500,000, more than three times the initial estimates
- A popular movie location, the Bradbury has appeared in *DOA* (1949), *Good Neighbor Sam* (1964), *Blade Runner* (1982), *Last Action Hero* (1993), *Murder in the First* (1994), *Lethal Weapon* (1998) and *Pay it Forward* (2000)

INFORMATION

- ✚ M7
- ✉ 304 S Broadway (access to the hallway only)
- ☎ 213/626–1893
- 🕐 Mon–Sat 9–5
- Ⓜ Civic Center
- 🚌 DASH D
- ♿ None
- 💵 Free
- ↔ Wells Fargo History Museum (➤ 36)
  Museum of Contemporary Art (➤ 37)
  Grand Central Market (➤ 38)
  California Plaza (➤ 54)
  Biltmore Hotel (➤ 56)

LITTLE TOKYO

The hub of LA's Japanese–American community, Little Tokyo is pleasantly low-key and walkable. There are surprise outposts of Japanese landscaping tucked into the concrete jungle and plenty of craft shops to nose around.

Historical footnotes Bounded by 1st and 3rd, Los Angeles and Alameda streets, this area was first settled at the end of the 19th century. Several historic buildings remain on 1st Street, which leads down to the Japanese American National Museum (▶ 50).

Sushi and *shiatsu* Over the road, among the neat green pompoms of pollarded trees and bright blue tile roofs, Japanese Village Plaza's 40 restaurants and small shops, exotic supermarkets, sushi bars and *shiatsu* massage parlours make for interesting browsing. You can then cross 2nd Street for the Japanese-American Cultural and Community Center, where the Doizaki Gallery exhibits Japanese artworks. The adjacent Japan America Theater presents contemporary and traditional Japanese performances such as Noh plays and Kabuki theatre productions. Outside, on Noguchi Plaza, a huge stone memorial commemorates the *Issei* (first generation Japanese-Americans).

Garden oasis Another feature of the plaza is the delightful James Irvine Garden, a Japanese-style oasis encircled by a stream, with paths, bridges, stepping stones, trees and flowering shrubs such as azaleas. There is more elegant Japanese landscaping nearby, outside the Higashi Hongwanji Buddhist Temple at No. 505 E 3rd Street, where dwarf pines, grassy tuffets and rock arrangements front the graceful neo-traditional façade.

EL PUEBLO DE LOS ANGELES

Angelenos tend to be snooty about the touristy Olvera Street market, but Sunday's mariachi masses in the Old Plaza Church are worthwhile, as are the more conventional historic sights.

LA's historic heart Wedged between Chinatown and Downtown, the site of the original 1781 pueblo settlement covers just a handful of city blocks. Within its confines are 27 historic buildings, including two museums, restaurants, shops and a Mexican street market. The main thoroughfare is pedestrianised Olvera Street, leading off La Placita, the former town plaza shaded by Moreton Bay fig trees. On the south side of the plaza be sure not to miss the original 1884 Firehouse No. 1, which displays antique firefighting equipment. The Old Plaza Church, on the west side, is the city's oldest Catholic church, dedicated in 1822.

Sterling support One of the oldest streets in the city, Olvera Street fell into disrepair around the turn of the century when the Downtown area moved south. By 1926, it was a grimy, mud-filled alley until local civic leader Christine Sterling stepped in. The story of Sterling's campaign to rescue the historic buildings and inaugurate the market in the 1930s is told in a display at the restored Avila Adobe.

Mexican marketplace Across the street, the Visitors Center in the 1887 Sepulveda House distributes walking tour maps, and shows a short video history of the city. Free guided walking tours leave from the Visitors Center. The market is still going strong, and the crowded thoroughfare is bursting with dozens of stalls selling everything from Mexican pottery and leatherware to sombreros.

DID YOU KNOW?

- Original settlement: Pueblo de Nuestra Señora la Reina de los Angeles (Our Lady Queen of the Angels)
- Oldest existing building: Avila Adobe (1818)
- The adobe (mud) walls of the Avila House are 3 feet thick
- The Avila House served as headquarters for Commodore Robert Stockton of the US Army during the Mexican–American War
- The Moreton Bay fig trees on the plaza were planted in the 1870s

INFORMATION

Visitors Center

- ✚ N6
- ✉ W-12 Olvera Street
- ☎ 213/628–1274
- 🕐 Mon–Sat 10–3
- 🚌 DASH B, D
- ♿ Few
- 🎫 Free
- ↔ Chinatown (▶ 17) Union Station (▶ 56)
- ❓ Walking tours Tue–Sat 10, 11 and noon Cinco de Mayo (5 May) and Dia de los Muertos (2 Nov) festivals (▶ 22)

Museums

- 🕐 Avila Adobe: Summer: daily 9–4. Winter: 10–4. Plaza Firehouse: Tue–Sun 10–3
- 🎫 Free

19

LONG BEACH & THE *QUEEN MARY*

The *Queen Mary*

- Launched: Clydeside, Scotland, 26 September 1934
- Portholes: 2,000-plus
- Gross tonnage: 81,237
- Passengers/crew: 1,957/1,174
- No. of transatlantic crossings: 1,001

INFORMATION

✚ Inside front cover
Long Beach Area Convention & Visitors Bureau
✉ One World Trade Center, Ocean Boulevard
☎ 562/436–3645
🕐 Mon–Fri 8:30–5
🚇 Metro Blue Line/Pacific Avenue
🅿 60
✋ Free

The *Queen Mary*
✉ Queen Mary Seaport, off I–710/Long Beach Freeway
☎ 562/435–3511
🕐 Daily 10:30–4:30
♿ Few
✋ Expensive

Aquarium of the Pacific
✉ 100 Aquarium Way
☎ 562/590–3100
🕐 Daily 9–6
♿ Very good
✋ Expensive

An easy day trip south from central Los Angeles, Long Beach has plenty to offer visitors – from the regal **Queen Mary** *and a jam-packed aquarium to watersports, shopping and gondola rides.*

On the water A convenient first stop at the foot of the freeway, the *Queen Mary* finally came to rest here in 1967. What was once the largest liner afloat is now a hotel, but regular guided tours give access to the engine rooms, cabin suites and gorgeous art deco salons. Across the Queensway Bay Bridge (water taxi service available), the excellent Aquarium of the Pacific showcases over 550 marine species from the northern Pacific to the tropics, including sharks, giant octopuses and California sea lions. East from here Shoreline Drive skirts San Pedro Bay, passing the Long Beach Arena encircled by the world's biggest mural, *Plant Ocean*, by the marine artist Wyland. Shoreline Village is popular for shopping and dining, with boat trips (▶ 19) and views of the *Queen Mary*.

Downtown to Venice Island Pine Avenue, at the heart of downtown Long Beach, bustles with shops and restaurants. Take Ocean Drive east to Belmont Shores, where concessionaires rent out watersports equipment, and bikes and skates for riding the beach path. Behind the beach 2nd Street is home to a mixed bag of shops and restaurants, and crosses on to Naples Island. This affluent residential neighbourhood, criss-crossed with canals, was developed in the 1920s. Explore it on foot, or indulge in a relaxing ride with Gondola Getaway (▶ 19).

RANCHO LOS ALAMITOS

This historic ranch house, which resides in the southeast section of Long Beach, brings a touch of the country to the heart of the city. The urban retreat grew up around the country's oldest domestic adobe (1806), and today thousands of visitors tour the house, its antique furnishings and lovely gardens.

Spanish land grant Now tucked away behind the gates of an exclusive residential development not far from Long Beach, the ranch house was once master of all it surveyed. The original 28,500-acre rancho was part of an enormous land grant allocated to a Spanish soldier, Manuel Nieto, in 1790. The Bixby family took possession of the property in 1881, and the house remained in the family for almost a century until it was donated to the City of Long Beach in 1968.

A family home The Bixbys were one of Southern California's most prominent pioneer ranching families, and Los Alamitos was the family home of Fred Bixby (1875–1952). From humble beginnings, the ranch house spread out on its hilltop site, and the views stretched across wheatfields to the ocean. During the 1920s and '30s, Fred's wife, Florence (1875–1961), set about developing the gardens, which are one of the highlights today. There is a distinctly Mexican-Mediterranean feel to the low white-washed walls and shaded walkways. Look for the lovely rose garden, an impressively spiky cacti collection and native Californian plantings. Tours of the house reveal that the original furnishings and family portraits are still in place. Five turn-of-the-century barns house a black-smith's shop, tackroom and stables with Shire draft horses. Children enjoy the sheep and goats, ducks, chickens, rabbits and doves.

DID YOU KNOW?

- The ranch occupies a hilltop 40 feet above sea level
- Gabrieleno Native Americans founded the village of Puvunga here in around AD 500
- Of Manuel Nieto's original 300,000-acre Spanish land grant, only 7.5 acres remain
- The first simple adobe shelter on this site was built around 1800
- The Moreton Bay fig on the property, its biggest tree, was planted in 1881

INFORMATION

- ✚ Inside back cover
- ✉ 6400 Bixby Hill Road (take 7th Street east; left on Studebaker Road; left on Anaheim)
- ☎ 562/431–3541
- 🕐 Wed–Sun 1–5 (last tour at 4)
- 🚌 LBT 42
- ♿ Few
- 🎫 Free
- ↔ Long Beach and the *Queen Mary* (➤ 42)
- ❓ Call for information about events and monthly Sunday afternoon education programmes (mostly free)

21

GAMBLE HOUSE

HIGHLIGHTS

- Front entrance: leaded glass by Emil Lange
- Main staircase
- Sitting room: carved reliefs of birds and plants
- Rugs from Greene and Greene designs
- Dining room furniture
- Tricks of the butler's pantry such as rollers for storing ironed tablecloths so that creases were never folded in to mar their perfection
- Guest bedroom: maple furnishings inlaid with silver

INFORMATION

- ✚ Inside back cover
- ✉ 4 Westmoreland Place, Pasadena (off N Orange Grove, just south of Rosemont)
- ☎ 626/793–3334
- ◷ Thu–Sun noon–3. Closed public hols
- 🚌 177, 267
- ♿ None
- 💰 Moderate
- ↔ Old Pasadena (➤ 18)
- ❓ Admission by guided tour only; frequent departures

The Gamble House takes the utilitarian California Bungalow and turns it into an art form. Every impeccably handcrafted inch of this superb American Arts and Crafts Movement house is a masterpiece.

The California Bungalow The Gamble House, designed by the architect brothers Charles and Henry Greene for David and Mary Gamble (of Procter and Gamble fame), is the most complete and well-preserved example of a handful of luxurious wooden 'bungalows' built in the first decade of the 20th century. The informal bungalow-style residence represented an appealing escape from Victorian stuffiness, and it was swiftly translated into Southern California's architectural vernacular.

A symphony in wood The Gamble House is, however, far from being a traditional bungalow. Greene and Greene's spreading two-storey design, with its Swiss- and Japanese-influenced lines, was planned in meticulous detail. The site was chosen to catch cool breezes from the Arroyo, and the arrangement of spacious verandas shaded by second-storey sleeping porches and overhanging eaves keeps the house comfortably ventilated. Working largely in wood, the Greenes cloaked the exterior with shingles and created a rich, golden timbered interior using Burmese teak, oak, maple, redwood and cedar. Every fixture and fitting, from the dining room furniture to the andirons in the fireplace, was custom-built, and many of the schemes were designed to complement Mary Gamble's favourite possessions such as Tiffany table lamps and opalescent Rockwood pottery. Architectural students and enthusiasts should not miss the excellent book shop, which also sells self-guided map tours around other Pasadena historic homes.

NORTON SIMON MUSEUM OF ART

If you have time to visit only one art museum in Los Angeles, make it the Norton Simon. Though its collections gathered here are not as well known as those in the Getty Center (▶ 25) and LACMA (▶ 30), it is superior to both in many ways.

Industrialist and collector The collections were originally founded as the Pasadena Art Institute in 1924. Under the direction of wealthy industrialist and collector Norton Simon (1907–93), the museum has grown into a world-class collection of European Old Master, Impressionist and Post-Impressionist works, as well as striking Asian sculpture, arranged in galleries around a lawned sculpture garden.

History of art The collections begin with jewel-like 14th-century Italian religious paintings and Renaissance art. The ravishing *Branchini Madonna* is just one of the highlights; the collection includes works by Filippino Lippi, Botticelli, Bellini and Cranach. From the 17th and 18th centuries there are Rembrandt portraits; Canaletto's minutely detailed Venetian scenes drawn with a master draftsman's skill; soft, plump Tiepolo figures; and Rubens's oils on a heroic scale. The superb 19th- to 20th-century galleries boast major works by Monet, Renoir, Cézanne and Van Gogh, and a fistful of colour from Matisse, Kandinsky, Braque and Klee. The superb Degas Collection numbers more than 100 pieces, including rare landscapes, enigmatic monotypes and an exceptional series of bronze dancers posthumously cast from wax models found in the artist's studio. The museum also possesses a rich collection of impressive Hindu and Buddhist sculpture from Nepal, India, Thailand and Cambodia.

HIGHLIGHTS

- *Branchini Madonna*, Giovanni di Paolo
- *Presumed Portrait of the Artist's Son, Titus*, Rembrandt
- *Burghers of Calais*, Rodin
- *The Stonebreakers*, Seurat
- *Exotic Landscape*, Rousseau
- *Flower Vendor*, Rivera
- *Odalisque with Tambourine*, Matisse
- *Woman with Book*, Picasso
- Degas Collection
- *The Mulberry Tree*, Van Gogh (below)

INFORMATION

- ✚ Inside back cover
- ✉ 411 W Colorado Boulevard, Pasadena
- ☎ 626/449–6840
- 🕐 Wed–Mon noon–6; Fri until 9
- 🚍 177, 180, 181
- ♿ Good
- 🍴 Moderate
- ↔ Old Pasadena (▶ 18)

23

THE HUNTINGTON

INFORMATION

- ✠ Inside back cover
- ✉ 1151 Oxford Road, San Marino (Pasadena)
- ☎ 626/405–2141
- ◷ Sep–May: Tue–Fri 12–4:30; Sat–Sun 10:30–4:30. Jun–Aug: Tue–Sun 10:30–4:30. Closed major hols
- 🍴 Restaurant and tea room
- 🚌 79, 379
- ♿ Good
- 🎟 Moderate. Free first Thu of month
- ↔ Old Pasadena (➤ 18)
  Gamble House (➤ 44)
  Norton Simon Museum of Art (➤ 45)
  Los Angeles State and County Arboretum (➤ 47)
- 🛈 Garden tours daily at 1

Above: Sarah Siddons as the Tragic Muse, *Sir Joshua Reynolds*

Three separate elements – manuscripts, paintings and gardens – contribute to the famously rich and varied Huntington experience, and there hardly seems enough time to do each of them justice.

Collections Henry E Huntington (1850–1927) moved to LA in 1902 and made a second fortune organising the city's rail system. When he retired to devote himself to his library, he married his uncle's widow, Arabella, who shared his interest in art. Together they amassed the 18th-century British portraits and French furnishings and decorative arts, setting up a trust bequeathing them for public benefit in 1919.

Manuscripts The Library building's extraordinary treasury of rare and precious manuscripts and books spans 800 years, from the famous 13th-century Ellesmere Chaucer to handwritten drafts of novels and poems by, for example, William Blake, Walt Whitman and Jack London.

Fine art The 1910 Beaux-Arts mansion, by Myron Hunt and Elmer Grey, displays the famous portrait collection, including Gainsborough's *Blue Boy*. Here too you will find ornate French furnishings and porcelain, and 18th-century European paintings added since Huntington's day. The Virginia Steele Scott Gallery houses recent acquisitions of American art from the 18th to early 20th centuries, and furnishings from the Arts and Crafts Movement team Greene and Greene (➤ 44).

Glorious gardens Huntington began work on the 150 acres of spectacular gardens in collaboration with William Hertrich in 1904. Today, there are approximately 15,000 types of plants and trees in 15 separate garden areas. The camellia woods are at their peak in spring, the rose garden in summer.

LA STATE & COUNTY ARBORETUM

Set against the backdrop of the San Gabriel Mountains, these lovely gardens in a corner of the old Rancho Santa Anita offer year-round colour and interest. Unwind amid this 127-acre parcel.

Mexican rancho Rancho Santa Anita was one of several ranches in the valley when Hugo Reid built his adobe house here in 1839. Furnished in simple pioneer style, it is one of three historic buildings in the grounds. The others are silver mining millionaire E J 'Lucky' Baldwin's fairytale 1881 Victorian cottage, and the 1890 Santa Anita Railroad Depot.

From *Acacia* to *Ziziphus* The lush profusion of trees and plants (the arboretum is a favourite exotic movie location) includes exuberant jungle areas, towering palms, splashing waterfalls and quiet corners to enjoy the peace – as long as the raucous peacocks are silent. Seek out the aquatic garden, the tropical greenhouse, the demonstration home gardens and the California landscape area, which shows the valley's natural state. There is much to see, so consider taking a tram tour to the further reaches of the grounds.

DID YOU KNOW?

- 36,000 plants from 5,000 species grow in the gardens
- 15,000-plus handmade bricks were used to construct the Hugo Reid Adobe, a California Historic Landmark
- 25 different types of palm tree grow in LA. The most common is the Mexican fan palm, the rarest *Jabaeopsis Caffra*, grown in the arboretum
- Scenes for the Humphrey Bogart–Katharine Hepburn movie *The African Queen* (1951) were filmed in the tropical gardens

INFORMATION

- ✚ Inside back cover
- ✉ 301 N Baldwin Road, Arcadia (off I–210/Foothill Freeway)
- ☎ 626/821–3222
- 🕐 Daily 9–5 (last ticket sales 4:30). Closed Christmas
- 🍴 Coffee shop
- 🚌 78, 79, 268
- ♿ Few
- 👤 Moderate
- ↔ Old Pasadena (➤ 18) Gamble House (➤ 44) Norton Simon Museum of Art (➤ 45) Huntington Library, Art Collections and Botanical Gardens (➤ 46)
- ❓ Regular tram tours visit the extensive grounds

Queen Anne guest house

DISNEYLAND

HIGHLIGHTS

- Jungle Cruise (Adventureland)
- Big Thunder Mountain Railroad (Frontierland)
- Honey, I Shrunk the Audience (Tomorrowland)
- Pirates of the Caribbean (New Orleans Square)
- Splash Mountain (Critter Country)
- Star Tours (Tomorrowland)

INFORMATION

- ✚ Inside back cover
- ✉ 1313 Harbor Boulevard (off I–5/Santa Ana Freeway), Anaheim
- ☎ 714/781–4565
- ⊙ Daily. Call for schedules. Approximate hours peak season 9AM–midnight or 1AM. Low season Mon–Fri 10–6; Sat 9–midnight; Sun 9–10PM
- 🍴 Snack bars, cafés and restaurants
- 🚃 460
- ♿ Excellent
- ✋ Very expensive (all rides and shows inclusive)
- ❓ Call ahead for details of nighttime shows and special holiday events

Since Disneyland opened its doors in 1955, Disney theme parks have become a world-wide phenomenon. The 80 acres offer a beguiling combination of more than 60 attractions, together with favourite Disney cartoon characters. Even if you've seen other Disney parks, don't miss the original.

Magic Kingdom Brilliantly conceived and operated like Swiss clockwork, the self-proclaimed 'Happiest Place on Earth' remains a perennial winner. Disney's particular brand of fantasy appeals across almost all age and cultural barriers. The park is divided into eight individually themed 'lands'. The gates open on to Main Street USA, a pastiche Victorian street lined with shops, which leads to the hub of the park at Sleeping Beauty Castle. From here you can explore the tropically inspired Adventureland, home to the rattling rollercoaster ride Indiana Jones™ Adventure, or take a turn around Wild West-style Frontierland. Small children favour the simpler, often cartoon-like rides in Fantasyland and Mickey's Toontown, while New Orleans Square has the ostentatious Haunted Mansion. Tomorrowland, now a vision of the future as seen in the past, stars mini space-ships and planet models, Rocket Rods XPR (Disneyland's fastest and longest ride to date) and the perennially popular Space Mountain all-in-the-dark rollercoaster.

Think ahead Getting the best out of Disneyland calls for advance planning. From July to early September, and in holiday periods, the park is very crowded and queues can be long. Weekends are especially busy (Sundays tend to be less crowded than Saturdays). Arrive early (the ticket office opens 30 minutes before the park) and make a dash for the best rides.

Top: Sleeping Beauty Castle

LOS ANGELES'
best

MUSEUMS

La Brea tar pits

Oozing from a fissure in the earth's crust, these gooey black tar pits are one of the world's most famous fossil sites. For thousands of years plants, birds and animals have been trapped and entombed here, turning the asphalt into a paleontological soup from which scientists have recovered millions of fossilised remnants from some 420 species of animal and 140 types of plant. Most of the fossils date from 10,000 to 40,000 years ago.

➕ Off map, west

✉ George C Page Museum of La Brea Discoveries, 801 Wilshire Boulevard, Midtown

☎ 323/934–7243

🕐 Daily 10–5 🚌 20, 21, 22, 217, 320

♿ Good 💲 Moderate

The splendid glass dome of the Natural History Museum of Los Angeles County

BANNING RESIDENCE MUSEUM

Entrepreneur and 'father of Los Angeles transportation', Phineas Banning (1830–85) built this grand Greek Revival mansion in 1864. Splendid Colonial furnishings, a 19th-century carriage barn and a park for picnicking.

➕ Off map, south ✉ 401 East M Street, Wilmington (off I–110/Harbor Freeway) ☎ 310/548–7777 🕐 Tue–Thu 12:30–2:30; Sat–Sun 12:30–3:30. Tours every hour 🚌 232 ♿ None 💲 Inexpensive

CALIFORNIA SCIENCE CENTER

Dozens of hands-on science, technology and environmental displays designed to appeal to children, plus an IMAX theatre.

➕ J11 ✉ 700 State Drive, Exposition Park ☎ 213/744–7400 🕐 Daily 10–5. Call for IMAX schedules 🚌 DASH F/Expo Park ♿ Very good 💲 Free (except IMAX theatre)

JAPANESE AMERICAN NATIONAL MUSEUM

The story of Japanese migration to the US, and the Japanese-Americans' struggle for acceptance in their adopted home. Moving exhibits deal with the World War II isolation camps.

➕ N7 ✉ 369 E 1st Street ☎ 213/625–0414 🕐 Tue–Sun 10–5; Thu until 8 🚌 DASH A ♿ Good 💲 Inexpensive

LOS ANGELES MARITIME MUSEUM

The largest maritime museum on the Pacific coast overlooks the busy Port of Los Angeles. There are dozens of beautifully crafted model ships, art, seafaring relics and real ships to visit.

➕ Off map, south ✉ Berth 84 (end of 6th
Street), San Pedro ☎ 310/548–7618
🕐 Tue–Sun 10–5 🚌 447 ♿ Good
✋ Inexpensive

MUSEUM OF NEON ART
This one-of-a-kind museum
displays vintage neon signs and
contemporary neon sculptures, and
offers monthly night-time tours of
LA's finest neon.
➕ L8 ✉ 501 W Olympic Boulevard
☎ 213/489–9918 🕐 Wed–Sat 11–5; Sun
noon–5 🚌 DASH C, E ♿ Few ✋ Inexpensive

MUSEUM OF TELEVISION AND RADIO
This tribute to more than 70 years
of home entertainment investigates
aspects of broadcasting from news
to *Star Trek* make-up.
➕ Off map, west ✉ 465 N Beverly Drive,
Beverly Hills ☎ 310/786–1000 🕐 Wed–Sun
noon–5; Thu until 9 🚌 3, 4 ♿ Good ✋ Inexpensive

PACIFIC ASIA MUSEUM
Notable Far Eastern art is displayed in rotation
alongside visiting exhibitions in an exotic 1920s
interpretation of a Chinese imperial palace.
➕ Off map, northeast ✉ 46 N Los Robles Avenue, Pasadena
☎ 626/449–2742 🕐 Wed–Sun 10–5; Thu until 8 🚌 180, 181,
188, 256, 260, 401 ♿ Few ✋ Inexpensive

RICHARD NIXON LIBRARY & BIRTHPLACE
This tribute to the 37th president includes his
televised debates with JFK, a collection of *Time
Magazine* covers featuring Nixon and snippets of
Watergate tapes.
➕ Off map, southwest ✉ 18001 Yorba Linda Boulevard, Yorba Linda
☎ 714/993–5075 🕐 Mon–Sat 10–5; Sun 11–5 ♿ Good
✋ Moderate

RONALD REAGAN PRESIDENTIAL LIBRARY & MUSEUM
After making a name for himself as an actor,
Ronald Reagan went on to serve as governor of
California before becoming the 40th president.
Peruse his filmography, photographs, presidential
gifts and papers; all on a 100-acre site.
➕ Off map, northwest ✉ 40 Presidential Drive, Simi Valley
☎ 805/522–8444 🕐 Daily 10–5 ♿ Good ✋ Moderate

SOUTHWEST MUSEUM
One of the finest collections of Native American
art and artefacts in the country; pity about the
somewhat lacklustre displays.
➕ Off map, north ✉ 234 Museum Drive (Avenue 43 exit off
I-110/Pasadena Freeway) ☎ 323/221–2164 🕐 Tue–Sun 10–5
🚌 81, 83 ♿ Few ✋ Inexpensive

Mona, by Lili Lakich, in the Museum of Neon Art

Beit Hashoah (House of the Holocaust)
Opened in 1993, less than a year
after the LA riots (➤ 12), the
Museum of Tolerance focuses its
attentions on both the dynamics
of prejudice and racism in
America, and the history of the
Holocaust. High-tech interactive
and experiential exhibits offer a
challenging insight into the
machinations of bigotry. World
War II artefacts and documents on
the second floor provide the most
moving memorial of all.
➕ Off map, west
✉ 9 Simon Wiesenthal Center,
786 W Pico Boulevard West LA
☎ 310/553–8403
🕐 Mon–Thu 10–4; Fri 10–3
(Nov–Mar until 1PM); Sun
10:30–5 🚌 SM7
♿ Very good ✋ Moderate 51

TV & MOVIE BUFF STUFF

See Top 25 Sights for
HOLLYWOOD BOULEVARD (▶ 31)
UNIVERSAL STUDIOS (▶ 32)

Grave affair

For years a mysterious veiled lady in black brought flowers to Rudolph Valentino's vault at Hollywood Memorial Park Cemetery, 6000 Santa Monica Boulevard, Hollywood, on the anniversary of his death. Others come to visit Cecil B De Mille, Tyrone Power and Douglas Fairbanks Sr. Buster Keaton, Stan Laurel and Bette Davis are among those buried at Forest Lawn Memorial Park, 6300 Forest Lawn Drive. Marilyn Monroe, Natalie Wood and Roy Orbison are at Westwood Memorial Park, 1218 Glendon Avenue.

Forest Lawn Memorial Park

BROADWAY HISTORIC THEATER DISTRICT

For movie fans with an interest in the early days, Downtown Broadway is the place to find the fabulous movie palaces of yesteryear. Several, such as the Los Angeles (No. 615), the Palace (No. 630) and the Orpheum Theater, are still open. Guided walk tours are available with the Los Angeles Conservancy (▶ 19).

➕ M7–8 ✉ Broadway, between 3rd and 9th streets
🚇 Pershing Square 🚌 27, 28, 45, 46

ENTERTAINMENT INDUSTRY DEVELOPMENT CORPORATION

If you want to see moviemakers on location, pick up a free copy of the daily shoot sheet from the sixth-floor permit office. It lists every motion picture, television programme, commercial and video being shot in the streets of the city that day.

➕ D1 ✉ 7083 Hollywood Boulevard, Hollywood ☎ 323/957–1000
🕐 Mon–Fri 8–6 🚌 1, 217

FREDERICK'S OF HOLLYWOOD LINGERIE MUSEUM

This selection of star undergarments displays offerings from Marilyn Monroe, Ingrid Bergman, Zsa Zsa Gabor, Cher and Joan Collins. Further examples of Frederick's creative way with the female form include the cleavage-enhancing Depth Charge bra.

➕ D1 ✉ 6608 Hollywood Boulevard, Hollywood ☎ 323/466–8506
🕐 Mon–Fri 10–9; Sat 10–7; Sun 11–6 🚌 1 ♿ None 🎟 Free

HOLLYWOOD ENTERTAINMENT MUSEUM
Memorabilia, interactive exhibits, and backlot
tours offer a peek behind the scenes at this user-
friendly film and movie museum. Chart the
development of film technology and movie make-
up, listen to taped interviews with famous actors
and directors, create your own sound effects, and
venture aboard the original set for the bridge of
Star Trek's 'Starship Enterprise'.
➕ D1 ✉ 7021 Hollywood Boulevard, Hollywood ☎ 323/465–
7900 🕐 Thu–Tue 11–6 🚌 1, 217 ♿ Very good 🅿 Moderate

HOLLYWOOD ROOSEVELT HOTEL
A romantic rendezvous for Clark Gable and his
wife, Carole Lombard, where Errol Flynn
supposedly invented his own gin cocktail behind
the barber shop, and where David Niven slept in
the servants' quarters before his star was born, the
Roosevelt mounts a display of photos and
Hollywood memorabilia from film's early days
through the 1940s: of greatest interest to movie
buffs.
➕ D1 ✉ 7000 Hollywood Boulevard, Hollywood
☎ 323/466–7000 🕐 Daily 🚌 1 ♿ Few 🅿 Free

HOLLYWOOD STUDIO MUSEUM
Cecil B De Mille shot Hollywood's first full-
length movie in this old horse barn in 1913.
Moved from its site on Vine to the Paramount lot
across from the Hollywood Bowl, it now houses
film memorabilia and antique
moviemaking equipment.
➕ D1 ✉ 2100 N Highland Avenue, Hollywood
☎ 323/874–2276 🕐 Thu–Sun 11–4; Sat–Sun
11–3:45 🚌 420 ,426 ♿ Few 🅿 Inexpensive

TOURLAND
A two-and-a-half hour orgy of
titillating trivia delivered on cue as
passengers (known as 'bodies') are
chauffeur-driven (in a hearse) past
the former homes of the stars and
sites of murders, suicides, sexual
shenanigans and everyday deviancy
in LaLaLand. Reservations required.
➕ D1 ✉ Departs from Orchid Street at Hollywood
Boulevard (east side of Mann's Chinese Theater)
☎ 323/782–9562 🕐 Heavenly Tour daily 10, 1.
Haunted Hearse daily 7PM 🚌 1 ♿ None 🅿 Very expensive

WARNER BROTHERS STUDIO VIP TOUR
The best behind-the-scenes tour for the serious
movie buff. Small groups (reservations advised;
no children under 8) tour backlot sets, watch
actual productions in progress where possible,
and learn about the nitty-gritty of moviemaking.
➕ Off map, northwest ✉ 4000 Warner Boulevard, Burbank
☎ 818/954–1744 🕐 Mon–Fri 9–3 🚌 96 ♿ Few
🅿 Very expensive

Lights! Camera! Action!

Dozens of TV shows in search of
an audience give away free
tickets through agencies such as
Audience Associates
(☎ 323/467–4697) and
Audiences Unlimited
(☎ 818/506–0043). You
can also apply direct to CBS
Television City
(☎ 323/575–2458) for *The
Price is Right*; NBC Television
(☎ 818/840–3537) for *The
Tonight Show with Jay Leno*;
Paramount Studios
(☎ 323/956–5575) for *Frasier*;
and Warner Bros Studios
(☎ 818/954–1744) for *E.R.*

*Charlie Chaplin statue in
the Hollywood Roosevelt
Hotel*

LANDMARKS

Blots on the horizon

Two high-rise districts loom large on the horizon, though they fail to cut much of an architectural dash. At least Downtown can lay claim to the tallest building west of Chicago in the 73-storey Library Tower, 633 W 5th Street. In West LA, Century City's gleaming towers (access from Avenue of the Stars) make a pretty show of reflecting the sunset in their blank glass faces, but the office-shopping-entertainment complex isn't architecturally inspiring. Century City is a hassle-free place to see movies and grab a bite.

Capitol Records Tower

ANGELS FLIGHT RAILWAY
From 1901 to 1969 the world's shortest railway (total length 315 feet) ferried passengers up and down Bunker Hill. Fully renovated and returned to service, the historic funicular shuttles between Hill Street and California Plaza like a small black and orange bug.
✚ M7 ✉ Hill Street at 4th Street ☎ 213/626–1901 🕐 Daily 6:30AM–10PM 💰 Inexpensive

CALIFORNIA PLAZA
Atop Bunker Hill, Downtown's towering concrete and glass financial district, the billion-dollar California Plaza complex (masterplan by Arthur Erikson Architects) houses offices, a hotel and MOCA (➤ 37). Be mesmerised by the dancing fountains, animated geysers that bounce and bubble to a multicoloured light show at night.
✚ M7 ✉ Grand Avenue 🚌 DASH B 💰 Free

CAPITOL RECORDS TOWER
Welton Becket's 1954 tower for the company that can list Frank Sinatra and the Beach Boys in its back catalogue is one of Hollywood's most famous landmarks. Though the architect denied it was intentional, it certainly looks like a stack of records topped by a needle.
✚ E1 ✉ 1750 Vine Street, Hollywood 🚌 1, 210, 310, 426

CITY HALL
This Downtown monolith, the tallest building in the city from 1928 until 1959, still cuts an imposing figure. Once 'destroyed' by Martians in *War of the Worlds*, it is familiar as the *Daily Planet* building in the *Superman* TV series, the police HQ from *Dragnet* and has starred in dozens of other TV series and films.
✚ N7 ✉ 200 N Spring Street 🚇 Civic Center 🚌 DASH D

COCA-COLA BOTTLING FACTORY
This 1936 streamlined Moderne triumph by Robert Derrah resembles a giant ocean liner with riveted port holes for windows, a 'bridge' structure bearing the Coca-Cola logo and a nautical red, white and blue trim.
✚ M10 ✉ 1334 S Central Avenue (at 14th Street) ☎ 213/746–5555 🚌 53

CRYSTAL CATHEDRAL
Close to Disneyland is Phillip Johnson's mega structure with a glass ceiling and walls.

🏠 Inside back cover ✉ 12141 Lewis Street, Garden Grove
☎ 714/971–4013 🕐 Tours Mon–Sat 9–3:30 ♿ None
✋ Inexpensive

FRANK GEHRY BUILDING ON MAIN
Formerly occupied by Chiat/Day Inc Advertising,
Frank Gehry's 1985 creation is definitely one for
the picture album. The entrance is flanked by a
pair of giant, three-storey high black binoculars
designed by Claes Oldenburg.
🏠 Off map, west ✉ 340 Main Street, Venice 🚌 33, 333, SM1

MANN'S CHINESE THEATER
A Hollywood legend in its own right, the Chinese
theatre was built by Sid Grauman in 1927 to host
extravagant premieres. The hodgepodge of
pagoda roofs and twiddly towers, dragon motifs,
Fu dogs and temple bells is appealingly kitsch,
and there is a splendid art-deco interior.
🏠 D1 ✉ 6925 Hollywood Boulevard, Hollywood
☎ 323/464–8111 🚌 1, 217

PACIFIC DESIGN CENTER
Beached just off La Cienega Boulevard,
this enormous coloured glass leviathan
(1975) is affectionately known as the 'Blue
Whale' for obvious reasons. Actually, there
are two buildings (one of them green) by
Cesar Pelli and Gruen Associates offering
a staggering 1.2 million square feet of
showroom space.
🏠 Off map, west ✉ 8687 Melrose Avenue (west of San
Vicente), West Hollywood ☎ 310/657–0800 🚌 10, 11

WATTS TOWERS
A bizarre beacon in this otherwise
run-down neighbourhood, these folk-art
towers were built from scrap by Italian
immigrant Simon Rodia between 1921
and 1954. Fashioned from steel rods, old
bed frames, bottles and more than 10,000
seashells, the central tower is almost 100
feet high. Visit the art centre next door.
🏠 Off map, south ✉ 1765 E 107th Street, Watts
☎ 213/847–4646 🕐 Closed for conservation

Hollywoodland
The famous Hollywood sign
derives from a 1923 promotion
when the word 'Hollywoodland'
was blazoned across the Hollywood Hills to sell a residential
development. The 'land' was
knocked off the sign in 1949, and
the remaining 50-foot high letters
are probably the city's most
recognisable landmark. There are
good views from high points all
over town, including the Griffith
Observatory (➤ 33).

*One of the towers at
Watts built from scrap*

HISTORIC BUILDINGS

See Top 25 Sights for
BRADBURY BUILDING (► 39)
EL PUEBLO DE LOS ANGELES, AVILA ADOBE
   (► 41)
GAMBLE HOUSE (► 44)

Mission survivors

Both LA's original Spanish missions still exist in the valleys that took their names. Southeast of Pasadena, the Mission San Gabriel Archangel, 428 S Mission Drive, San Gabriel (☎ 626/457–3048), was founded first in 1771. Although badly shaken by recent earthquakes, it is set in pretty gardens and the church has been reopened. The attractive Mission San Fernando Rey de España, at 15151 San Fernando Mission Boulevard, Mission Hills, (☎ 818/361–0186) appears in better condition, but has been largely reconstructed.

BILTMORE HOTEL

This grand old dame dates from 1923. Enter from Pershing Square to admire the beautifully restored Spanish Revival-style Rendezvous Court lobby.
✚ M7 ✉ 506 S Grand 🚇 Pershing Square 🚌 DASH B, C

ENNIS-BROWN HOUSE

The best of Frank Lloyd Wright's Maya-style concrete structures (1924) on a terrific site in the hills near Griffith Park. Tours only by reservation.
✚ Off map, northwest ✉ 2655 Glendower Avenue, Los Feliz
☎ 323/660–0607 🕐 Mon–Sat tours only 💰 Expensive

HOLLYHOCK HOUSE

LA's architectural treasure designed by Frank Lloyd Wright is under renovation until 2003. Visitors can explore its grounds at Barnsdall Art Park and peruse changing exhibits at the LA Municipal Art Gallery.
✚ H2 ✉ Barnsdall Park, 4800 Hollywood Boulevard, Hollywood
☎ 213/485–4581 🚌 1, 217 💰 Inexpensive

LOS ANGELES CENTRAL LIBRARY

A Beaux-Arts treasure (1926, Goodhue and Winslow Sr) ornamented with carved reliefs of great thinkers, writers, scientists and choice *bons mots*. Historic 1930s murals in the Cook Rotunda.
✚ M7 ✉ 630 W 5th Street ☎ 213/228–7000 🕐 Mon–Thu 10–8;
Fri–Sat 10–6; Sun 1–5. Tours Mon–Fri 12:30; Sat 11, 2; Sun 2
🚇 Pershing Square 🚌 DASH A, B, C, F ♿ Good 💰 Free

Rudolph Schindler's house

SCHINDLER HOUSE

Rudolph Schindler's innovative 1921 design for California living. Its indoor/outdoor plan became the prototype for much Southern California vernacular architecture.
✚ Off map, west ✉ 835 N Kings Road, West Hollywood ☎ 323/651–1510 🕐 Wed–Sun 11–6
♿ Few 💰 Moderate

UNION STATION

This Spanish Mission-style beauty was built by the railroad companies in 1939 (design by J and D Parkinson). View the lofty, barrel-shaped ceiling and Moorish tile trim of the main hall.
✚ N6/7 ✉ 800 N Alameda Street 🚇 Union Station
🚌 DASH B, D

GARDENS & GREEN SPACES

See Top 25 Sights for
GRIFFITH PARK (► 33)
**HUNTINGTON LIBRARY, ART COLLECTIONS
AND BOTANICAL GARDENS** (► 46)
**LOS ANGELES STATE AND COUNTY
ARBORETUM** (► 47)
RANCHO LOS ALAMITOS (► 43)

DESCANSO GARDENS
Glorious gardens covering 65 acres, including a
30-acre California live oak forest. Camellias
bloom spectacularly from January to March. (See
Pasadena Pops ► 82.)
🔲 Off map, northeast ✉ 1418 Descanso Drive, La Cañada (Verdugo
Boulevard exit off I-210/Foothill Freeway, northwest of Pasadena)
☎ 818/952–4400 🕐 Daily 9–4:30 except Christmas 🚌 177
🚻 Moderate

EXPOSITION PARK ROSE GARDEN
This fragrant spot boasts around 20,000 rose
bushes from some 200 varieties in a sunken
garden beside the Natural History Museum.
🔲 J11 ✉ 900 Exposition Boulevard 🕐 Open site 🚌 DASH
F/Expo Park 🚻 Free

GREYSTONE PARK
The parklands surrounding oil millionaire
Edward Doheny's 1928 Gothic mansion
offer fine views over Beverly Hills.
🔲 Off map, west ✉ 905 Loma Vista Drive, Beverly Hills
☎ 310/550–4654 🕐 Daily 10–5; until 6 in summer
🚌 2, 3, 302 🚻 Free

VIRGINIA ROBINSON MANSION &
GARDENS
A hidden treasure of Beverly Hills, the
late society hostess Virginia Robinson's
Mediterranean-style villa is set in 6 acres
of lush gardens and groves with palms,
terraces and water features.
🔲 Off map, west ✉ 1008 Elden Way, Beverly Hills
☎ 310/276–5367 🕐 Tue–Fri by reservation only
🚻 Moderate

WILL ROGERS STATE HISTORIC PARK
There is plenty of space for kids to run
wild and picnic on this 186-acre hillside
ranch, the Western-style home of the
'Cowboy Philosopher'. There are house
tours, a nature trail, and horses, stables and
occasional polo games to watch.
🔲 Off map, west ✉ 1501 Will Rogers State Park Road, off Sunset
Boulevard ☎ 310/454–8212 🕐 Park: daily 8–sunset. House: daily
10:30–3:30 🚌 2, 302 🚻 Moderate

Touring Eden
A landscape architect and a
landscape designer set up the
guide service Touring Eden
(☎ 818/769–2304) to squire
garden lovers around LA's
horticultural highlights. From
Malibu to Beverly Hills and up to
Pasadena, they offer expert and
enthusiastically guided tours for
individuals and groups.

*Virginia Robinson
Gardens*

57

ATTRACTIONS FOR CHILDREN

See Top 25 Sights for
AUTRY MUSEUM OF WESTERN HERITAGE (➤ 35)
DISNEYLAND (➤ 48)
GRIFFITH PARK (➤ 33)
NATURAL HISTORY MUSEUM OF LA COUNTY (➤ 34)
RANCHO LOS ALAMITOS (➤ 43)
UNIVERSAL STUDIOS (➤ 32)

Miniature marvels

Wilshire Boulevard's 'Miracle Mile' museums offer an interesting choice of attractions for kids, all within a couple of minutes' walk of each other. The fossils at the George C Page Museum (➤ 50) appeal to young paleontologists; the shiny automobiles of the Petersen Automotive Museum (➤ 29) to child racers; and the Carol & Barry Kaye Museum of Miniatures, 5900 Wilshire Boulevard, Midtown (☎ 323/937–6464), exercises a mesmerising doll's-house charm.

Shopfront detail, Hollywood Boulevard

HOLLYWOOD GUINNESS WORLD OF RECORDS MUSEUM

Trivia galore from The-Animal-with-the-Smallest-Brain-in-Proportion-to-Body-Size (a *Stegosaurus*) to the Most Biographed Female (Marilyn Monroe).
➕ D1 ✉ 6764 Hollywood Boulevard, Hollywood ☎ 323/463–6433 ⏰ Daily 10–midnight 🚌 1 💷 Moderate

KNOTT'S BERRY FARM

The nation's first theme park. Visit Camp Snoopy and the 1880s frontier Ghost Town; splash down in Wild Water Wilderness and ride the Jaguar roller coaster. Special Halloween programme.
➕ Off map, southeast ✉ 8039 Beach Boulevard, Buena Park ☎ 714/220–5200 ⏰ Call for schedules 🚌 460 💷 Very expensive

MUSEUM OF FLYING

The history of flight, vintage planes and interactive exhibits, including the first aircraft to circumnavigate the globe (in 1924).
➕ Off map, southwest ✉ 2772 N Donald Douglas Loop, Santa Monica Airport ☎ 310/392–8822 ⏰ Wed–Sun 10–5 🚌 SM8 💷 Moderate

PACIFIC PARK

A seaside fairground with traditional rides (➤ 24), sideshows and amusement arcades, plus virtual reality simulator adventures.
➕ Off map, west ✉ Santa Monica Pier, opposite Colorado Avenue ☎ 310/260–8744 ⏰ Seasonal schedules 🚌 20, 22, 33, SM1, 7, 10 💷 Charge per ride

SIX FLAGS CALIFORNIA

Santa Clarita Valley's theme park duo: Magic Mountain, renowned for its hair-raising thrill rides; and the Hurricane Harbor Water Park (summer season only).
➕ Off map, northwest ✉ Magic Mountain exit off I–5/Golden State Freeway ☎ 818/367–5965 ⏰ Call for schedules 🚌 Metrolink to Santa Clarita, then SCT30 💷 Very expensive

FREE ATTRACTIONS

Santa Monica beach and pier

CABRILLO AQUARIUM
Southern California marine life from the fantail sole known for its camouflage abilities to the bizarre grunion, a fish that comes ashore to breed.
🚇 Off map, south 📮 Stephen White Drive (off Pacific Avenue), San Pedro ☎ 310/548–7562 🕐 Tue–Fri noon–5; Sat–Sun 10–5 🚌 446

FRANKLIN D MURPHY SCULPTURE GARDEN
Sculptures by such artists as Arp, Hepworth and Calder are sprinkled liberally over sunny lawns shaded by jacaranda trees. Works by Henry Moore, Miró, Maillol and Rodin can be found on the tree-lined promenade.
🚇 Off map, west 📮 UCLA Campus off Circle Drive East, Westwood 🕐 Open site 🚌 2, 302, SM1, 2, 3, 8, 12 (off Sunset Boulevard)

MULHOLLAND DRIVE
This winding mountain road with terrific views runs from Hollywood west past Malibu (with an unpaved section through Topanga State Park). Access to the eastern section off Laurel Canyon Boulevard; to the western section from Old Topanga Canyon Road.

Take a tour
The West Coast's biggest newspaper, the *Los Angeles Times*, offers free behind-the-scenes tours of its offices on weekdays (☎ 213/237–5757); and there are free tours of the attractively landscaped UCLA campus at Westwood (☎ 310/825–8764). On Pasadena's 'Millionaires' Row', the Wrigley Gardens at Tournament House, 391 S Orange Grove Boulevard (☎ 626/449–4100), are open daily with free tours on Thursday afternoons from February to August.

BEACHES

See Top 25 Sights for
SANTA MONICA AND VENICE BEACH (➤ 24, 26)
LONG BEACH (➤ 42)

Hermosa Beach

Off the beaten track

It is no easy task to escape the crowds. However, there are a few relatively quiet corners, namely a handful of small coves tucked into the steep, rocky bluffs of the Palos Verdes peninsula. On the north side, beyond Redondo Beach, try sandy Malaga Cove. Around to the south, near Lloyd Wright's Wayfarer's Chapel, Abalone Cove's rock pools provide entertainment and there is some good snorkelling.

HERMOSA BEACH
Slipped in between the other two major South Bay beaches, Manhattan and Redondo, Hermosa is LA's leading party beach. Lots of hanging out and volleyball for the well-toned.
➕ Off map, southwest ✉ Off Pacific Coast Highway, Hermosa Beach 🚌 439

LEO CARRILLO STATE BEACH
On the LA County line north of Malibu. Broad, the mile-long sandy beach is divided by Sequit Point. You can surf to the north; paddle in tide pools; and explore underwater caves revealed at low tide.
➕ Off map, west ✉ Off Pacific Coast Highway (11 miles west of Malibu) 🚌 434

MALIBU SURFRIDER STATE BEACH
One of California's original surfing beaches (➤ 24), offers year-round waves but the best are during the late-summer southern swells (Aug–Sep).
➕ Off map, west ✉ Off Pacific Coast Highway, Malibu 🚌 434

MANHATTAN BEACH
Fashionable beach suburb with cafés along the seafront. Good swimming, surfing and games.
➕ Off map, southwest ✉ Manhattan Beach Boulevard (off Pacific Coast Highway) 🚌 439

REDONDO BEACH
Hotel-lined beach with good swimming and a heated lagoon for children. Fishing from the pier.
➕ Off map, southwest ✉ Off Pacific Coast Highway 🚌 439

WILL ROGERS STATE BEACH
Just north of Santa Monica, this is a good family beach with parking and fewer crowds.
➕ Off map, west ✉ Off Pacific Coast Highway (opposite Sunset Boulevard), Pacific Palisades 🚌 434

ZUMA BEACH
LA's biggest beach is hip and hot among San Fernando Valley girls (and boys). Crowded at weekends.
➕ Off map, west ✉ Off Pacific Coast Highway (6 miles west of Malibu) 🚌 434

LOS ANGELES
where to...

CALIFORNIA CUISINE

Prices

Average meal per person excluding drinks

£ up to $15
££ $15 to $30
£££ $30 to $50
££££ over $50

Except for luxury restaurants categorised as ££££, where dinner could easily cost upwards of $70 for two people excluding wine (lunch will be less; typically around $40), dining in LA need not cost an arm and a leg. If you eat in reasonable restaurants, anticipate spending around $6–$8 per person for breakfast, $10 for lunch, and $15–$20 for dinner excluding drinks. Wherever you dine, a tip of at least 15 per cent of the bill excluding wine is expected.

Opening times

All the listed restaurants are open daily for lunch and dinner unless otherwise stated. Angelenos generally lunch between 11:30 and 2, and have dinner between 6 and 9, though many restaurants open earlier and/or close later than these times.

CHAYA (£££)
Minimalist with a Japanese sensibility that's also evident in the innovative, intriguing East-meets-West menu.
✠ Off map, west ✉ 8741 Alden Drive, West Hollywood ☎ 310/859–8833 🕐 Dinner only at weekends 🚇 14, 16

CHINOIS ON MAIN (££££)
Another bustling and stylish showcase for chef Wolfgang Puck's sensational California-Chinese creations.
✠ Off map, west ✉ 2709 Main Street, Santa Monica ☎ 310/392–9025 🕐 Lunch Wed–Fri; dinner daily 🚇 33, SM1

CITRUS (£££)
Superstar-chef Michel Richard's casually chic American bistro offers creative, US versions of French classics.
✠ D3 ✉ 6703 Melrose Avenue ☎ 323/857–0034 🕐 Lunch Mon–Fri; dinner daily 🚇 10, 11

FENIX (£££)
Stunning art-deco decor plus views and inventive California/French menu. Check out the jazz night.
✠ Off map, west ✉ Argyle Hotel, 8358 Sunset Boulevard, ☎ 323/848–6677 🕐 Lunch, dinner Mon–Sat; lunch Sun 🚇 2, 3

JIRAFFE (£££)
California-bistro fare, served in airy space, and casually chic two-storey dining room.
✠ Off map, west ✉ 502 Santa Monica Boulevard, Santa Monica ☎ 310/917–6671 🕐 Lunch Tue–Fri; dinner daily 🚇 SM4

MICHAEL'S (£££)
A California culinary pioneer, with an impressive contemporary art collection and lovely terrace.
✠ Off map, west ✉ 1147 3rd Street, Santa Monica ☎ 310/451–0843 🕐 Lunch, dinner Mon–Fri 🚇 20, 33, SM2

PARKWAY GRILL (£££)
Cutting-edge California fare with Southwestern accents.
✠ Off map, northeast ✉ 510 S Arroyo Parkway, Pasadena ☎ 626/795–1001 🕐 Lunch Mon–Fri; dinner daily 🚇 401, 402

THE RAYMOND (£££)
Pretty, historic California bungalow with patios and a mixed menu.
✠ Off map, northeast ✉ 1250 S Fair Oaks Avenue, Pasadena ☎ 626/441–3136 🕐 Tues–Sun 🚇 483

SPAGO (£££)
Chef Wolfgang Puck's celebrity-studded haunt. Fine California cuisine includes the famous (but pricey) designer pizza.
✠ Off map, west ✉ 1114 Horn Avenue, West Hollywood ☎ 310/652–4025 🕐 Dinner daily 🚇 2, 3

SPAGO OF BEVERLY HILLS (££££)
The Beverly Hills outpost of Wolfgang Puck's legendary chain remains the premier place to rub elbows with the rich and famous. Atmosphere pure LA.
✠ Off map, west ✉ 176 N Canon Drive, ☎ 310/385–0880 🕐 Lunch Mon–Sat; dinner daily 🚇 20, 21, 22, 320

STEAK/SEAFOOD/HEARTY FARE

CHEF JAY (££)

Sawdust and peanut shells litter the floor, but it's all part of the charm at this restaurant-cum-watering hole that dishes fresh surf-and-turf. First opened in 1959.

🞧 Off map west ✉ 1657 Ocean Avenue Santa Monica ☎ 310/395–1741 🕐 Breakfast Sat, Sun; lunch, dinner daily 🚌 4, 20, 22, SM1, 1, 2, 3, 7, 8, 9, 10

THE IVY (£££)

Reservations are a must for this film-folk hang-out. Try the white-chocolate lemon and walnut cake. Terrace dining.

🞧 Off map, west ✉ 113 N Robertson Boulevard, West Hollywood ☎ 310/274–8303 🚌 14, 16

LAWRY'S THE PRIME RIB (£££)

Aged prime rib, Yorkshire pudding, creamed spinach and horseradish sauce. Clubby surroundings; established in 1938.

🞧 Off map, west ✉ 100 N La Cienega Boulevard, Beverly Hills ☎ 310/652–2827 🕐 Dinner daily 🚌 20, 21, 22, 105

MCCORMICK & SCHMICK'S (££)

Downtown outpost of a popular chain of attractive, traditional-style fish restaurants.

🞧 L7 ✉ Library Tower, 633 W 5th Street (4th floor) ☎ 213/629–1929 🕐 Lunch, dinner Mon–Fri; dinner Sat, Sun 🚌 DASH B, C, D

MORTON'S (£££)

Stylish film-industry favourite packed with celebs grazing from the slightly healthy American menu.

🞧 Off map, west ✉ 8764 Melrose Avenue, West Hollywood ☎ 310/276–5205 🕐 Lunch, dinner Mon–Fri; dinner Sat 🚌 10

PACIFIC DINING CAR (££–£££)

This railway-theme restaurant offers superb steaks around the clock. Good selection of fish and shellfish.

🞧 L7 ✉ 1310 W 6th Street ☎ 213/483–6000 🕐 24 hours daily 🚌 18, 20, 21, 200

REEL INN (££)

Casual, beachy vibe where diners share picnic tables while eating just-out-of-the-ocean seafood. Generous portions; no waiters.

🞧 Off map west ✉ 1220 Third Street Promenade, Santa Monica ☎ 310/395–5538 🚌 4, 20, 22, SM1, 2, 3, 7, 8, 9, 10

SADDLE PEAK LODGE (£££)

Rustic and romantic hunting lodge hideaway in the Santa Monica Mountains. Excellent game dishes in season.

🞧 Off map, northwest ✉ 419 Cold Canyon Road, Calabasas (San Fernando Valley) ☎ 310/456–7325 🕐 Brunch Sun; dinner Wed–Sun

WATER GRILL (££)

Renowned seafood restaurant with oyster bar.

🞧 M7 ✉ 544 S Grand Avenue, Downtown ☎ 213/891–0900 🕐 Lunch, dinner Mon–Fri; dinner Sat, Sun 🚌 DASH B, E

California or Californian?

When visiting the US you find that Americans rarely use the adjective Californian. This is generally reserved only when referring to the Californian people but as a rule you will see California in front of most words, such as California wine and California cuisine.

California cuisine

Fresh, seasonal, inventive and health-conscious. These words help define California cuisine, the cooking style launched in 1971 by celebrity chef Alice Waters in the kitchen of her lauded Berkely, California restaurant, Chez Panisse. The approach caught on throughout the state, with chefs learning to take advantage of seasonal ingredients and appreciate nature's bounty. An autumn menu, for example, might include a salad tossed with fall nuts, butternut squash soup and pumpkin risotto.

FRENCH & ITALIAN

California drinking

California wines make a fine accompaniment to almost any meal. Most come from the 400 or so wineries located in the Napa and Sonoma valleys north of San Francisco, where common grape varieties include Cabernet Sauvignon and Chardonnay, as well as California's unique varietal, Zinfandel, used to produce red, white and pink wines. Winemakers' names to watch for include Murphy-Goode, Carmenet, Gundlach-Bundschu, Niebaum-Coppola, Inglenook, Lytton Springs, Ridge and also the *méthode champenoise* sparkling wines from Domaine Chandon.

FRENCH

THE DINING ROOM (£££)

Beautiful formal dining room serving elegant cuisine. Lengthy wine list and an excellent, polished service.

➕ Off map, west ✉ Regent Beverly Wilshire Hotel, 9500 Wilshire Boulevard, Beverly Hills ☎ 310/274–8179 🚌 20, 21, 22

L'ORANGERIE (£££)

Grand French restaurant with palatial decor, great service and a classic menu. Terrace dining.

➕ Off map, west ✉ 903 N La Cienega Boulevard, West Hollywood ☎ 310/652–9770 🕐 Dinner Tue–Sun 🚌 4, 105

PATINA (£££)

Exceptional modern French cuisine in a relaxed setting. Chef Joachim Splichal is probably the brightest star in LA's culinary firmament.

➕ E3 ✉ 5955 Melrose Avenue, Hollywood ☎ 323/467–1108 🕐 Lunch Tue–Sun; dinner daily 🚌 10

PINOT BISTRO (£££)

Try the interesting, well executed French bistro fare at famed chef Joachim Splichal's quaint restaurant.

➕ Off map, west ✉ 12969 Ventura Boulevard, Studio City ☎ 818/990–0500 🕐 Lunch Mon–Fri; dinner daily 🚌 218, 424, 522, 425

TWIN PALMS (££)

Named for the huge trees that poke out of the dining room into the sky, this country French restaurant continues to impress diners. Live music at weekends.

➕ Off map, northwest ✉ 101 West Green Street, Pasadena ☎ 626/577–2567 🚌 Pasadena buses 180, 181 and local shuttle

ITALIAN

ANGELI CAFFE (££)

Locals love the antipasto as well as the wood-oven pizza at this hip and friendly restaurant.

➕ C3 ✉ 7274 Melrose Avenue ☎ 323/936–9086 🕐 Lunch Mon–Sat; dinner daily 🚌 10, 11

DRAGO (££-£££)

Celestino Drago delivers mouth-watering Italian fare to an affluent crowd at his casual flagship restaurant. Regulars favour Sicilian dishes.

➕ Off map, west ✉ 2628 Wilshire Boulevard, Santa Monica ☎ 310/828–1585 🕐 Lunch Mon–Fri; dinner daily 🚌 20, 320

LOCANDA VENETA (£££)

Simple northern Italian cuisine in a robust, lively setting. Try a booth.

➕ Off map, west ✉ 8638 W Third Street ☎ 310/274–1893 🕐 Lunch Mon–Fri; dinner Mon–Sat 🚌 16, 220

VALENTINO (£££)

Piero Selvaggi provides heavenly cuisine and an extensive wine list with white-glove service. A top dining choice.

➕ Off map, west ✉ 3115 Pico Boulevard, Santa Monica ☎ 310/829–4313 🕐 Lunch Fri; dinner Mon–Sat 🚌 SM7, 14

ASIAN

CHAN DARA (£–££)
Small, trendy Thai dining room. Spicy soups and curries, satay and good noodles.
✉ 1511 N Cahuenga Boulevard, Hollywood ☎ 323/464–8585 🕐 Lunch Mon–Fri; dinner daily 🚌 2, 3

GINZA SUSHI (££££)
This temple of Japanese gastronomy probably offers the most exciting sushi experience outside of Japan – worth every cent of the outrageously high price tag. Surrender to the whims of chef Masa Takayama and you are in for a notable meal.
✚ Off map, west ✉ 218 Via Rodeo, Beverly Hills ☎ 310/247–8939 🕐 Dinner Tue–Sat 🚌 20, 21, 22, 320

JOSS (££)
Sleek Chinese restaurant serving several unusual specialities such as Mongolian lamb.
✚ Off map, west ✉ 9255 Sunset Boulevard, Hollywood ☎ 310/276–1886 🕐 Lunch Mon–Fri; dinner daily 🚌 2, 3

KATSU 3RD (£££)
Top notch, melt-in-your-mouth sushi. Minimalist decor.
✚ Off map, west ✉ 8638 W Third Street ☎ 310/273–3605 🕐 Lunch, Mon–Fri; dinner daily 🚌 26, 204

LE COLONIAL (£££)
French-Vietnamese fare in stylised Saigon atmosphere. Consistently busy.
✚ Off map, west ✉ 8783 Beverly Boulevard, W Hollywood ☎ 310/289–0660 🚌 14, 220

OCEAN SEAFOOD (££)
Vast Cantonese restaurant serving affordable fresh seafood dishes and dim sum among other favourites.
✚ N6 ✉ 747 N Broadway ☎ 213/687–3088 🚌 DASH B

SEOUL JUNG (£££)
Exquisite Korean cuisine, including traditional barbecue prepared at the table. Luxurious atmosphere, solicitous service.
✚ L7 ✉ Wilshire Grand Hotel, 930 Wilshire Boulevard ☎ 213/688–7777 🚌 18, 20, 21, 200

THOUSAND CRANES (£££)
Fine Japanese cuisine, sushi and *tempura* counters, charming service and views over a Japanese garden.
✚ N7 ✉ New Otani Hotel, 120 S Los Angeles Street, Little Tokyo ☎ 213/253–9255 🕐 Lunch Sun–Fri; dinner daily 🚌 DASH A

WOO LAE OAK OF SEOUL (££)
Modern Korean cooking, finally out of Koreatown, melds Korean and French flavours.
✚ Off map, west ✉ 170 N La Cienega Boulevard, Beverly Hills ☎ 310/652–4187 🚌 20, 21, 22, 105

YUJEAN KANG'S (££)
Chef Yujean Kang creates intriguing Chinese cuisine, with such dishes as 'pictures in the snow'.
✚ Off map, northeast ✉ 67 North Raymond Avenue, Pasadena ☎ 626/585–0855 🚌 187

Snack stops

Dim sum (Chinese dumplings) and noodle dishes make an inexpensive lunchtime treat at notable dim sum parlours as Chinatown's Mandarin Deli ✉ 727 N Broadway, or Grandview Gardens ✉ 944 N Hill Street. Don't expect menus – instead, the waiters continuously stop by your table with different dishes, and you make your selections. For an affordable sushi blowout, make tracks for the all-you-can-eat sushi counter at Lighthouse Buffet ✉ 201 Arizona Avenue, Santa Monica.

MEXICAN & SOUTHWESTERN

A-maizing

Ground corn (*maíz* in Spanish) is a Mexican staple, and the chief ingredient of *tortillas*, the ubiquitous cornmeal pancakes that turn up in any number of guises on Mexican menus. Some of the most common varieties are soft, folded *burritos*, deep-fried *enchiladas*, crescent-shaped, deep-fried *quesadillas* filled with cheese and chillies (a useful vegetarian option) and crispy folded *tacos* (*taco* literally means 'snack' in Mexico).

AUTHENTIC CAFE (£–££)
At this highly popular café sprinkled with New Mexican paraphernalia long queues build. The draw is Southwestern fare that is delicious, inventive and authentic. Friendly.
➕ Off map, south ✉ 7605 Beverly Boulevard, Melrose-La Brea ☎ 323/939–4626 🚌 14, 212

BARNEY'S BEANERY (£–££)
Friendly roadhouse-style diner serving generous portions of Tex-Mex fare and hamburgers plus a lengthy beer menu, a bar and two pool tables.
➕ Off map, west ✉ 8447 Santa Monica Boulevard, West Hollywood ☎ 323/654–2287 🚌 4

BORDER GRILL (££)
Great Mexican food with an inventive twist and a loud, eclectic crowd. Always packed.
➕ Off map, west ✉ 1445 4th Street, Santa Monica ☎ 310/451–1655 🚌 4, SM1, 7, 10

EL CHOLO (££)
LA institution (est 1927) serving great Mexican fare in hacienda-style surroundings with patio tables.
➕ Off map, west ✉ 1121 S Western Avenue, Midtown ☎ 323/734–2773 🚌 30, 31

EL TORITO GRILL (££)
Busy, fun place offering a wide range of Mexican and Southwestern dishes washed down with tequila.
➕ Off map, west ✉ 9595 Wilshire Boulevard, Beverly Hills ☎ 310/550–1599 🚌 20, 21, 22

KAY 'N DAVE'S (£–££)
Great value meals in this cheerful, unpretentious neighbourhood restaurant. Great *mole*.
➕ Off map, west ✉ 262 26th Street, Santa Monica ☎ 310/459–8118 🚌 SM4, 20

LA GOLONDRINA (££)
Classic Mexican joint in El Pueblo. *Mariachi* musicians and margaritas.
➕ N6 ✉ W 17 Olvera Street ☎ 213/628–4349 🚇 Union Station 🚌 DASH B

REBECCA'S (£££)
Push through the crowded bar to get to your table. Cuisine is *Nueva Mexicana*.
➕ Off map, west ✉ 101 Broadway, Santa Monica ☎ 310/260–1100 🚌 SM1, SM8

SONORA CAFÉ (£££)
Sophisticated South-western cuisine and home-on-the-range decor.
➕ Off map, west ✉ 180 S La Brea Avenue, Midtown ☎ 213/857–1800 🕐 Lunch Mon–Fri; dinner daily 🚌 14

TEX-MEX PLAYA (£–££)
Cheery margarita-fuelled Tex-Mex *cantina* on the beach at Pacific Palisades.
➕ Off map, west ✉ 118 Entrada Drive, Santa Monica ☎ 310/459–8596 🚌 434

MISCELLANEOUS SELECTION

BOMBAY CAFÉ (££)

An increasingly gentrified and pleasant neighbourhood is home to this highly regarded Indian spot known for flavourful, spicy dishes.

✚ Off map, west
✉ 12021 W Pico Boulevard
☎ 310/473–3388 ◷ Lunch, Mon–Fri; dinner daily
🚌 30, 31, SM7

DAR MAGHREB (£££)

Forgo utensils while dining on Moroccan fare accompanied by belly dancers. Multi-course, *prix-fixe* dinner.

✚ B2 ✉ 7651 Sunset Boulevard, West Hollywood
☎ 323/876–7651
◷ Dinner daily 🚌 2, 3

DC3 (££)

California cuisine for plane-lovers. Fresh pasta, grilled seafood and uninterrupted runway views.

✚ Off map, southwest
✉ 2800 Donald Douglas Loop North, Santa Monica Airport
☎ 310/399–2323
◷ Lunch, Mon–Fri; dinner Tue–Sat 🚌 SM8

DIAGHILEV (££££)

A formal, Russian-French classic with a Belle Epoque interior; draws favour for its exquisite caviar and updated Russian fare.

✚ Off map, west ✉ Wyndham Bel Age Hotel, 1020 N San Vincente Boulevard, West Hollywood ☎ 310/854–1111
◷ Dinner Tue–Sat 🚌 2, 3

FIG TREE (££)

Fresh grilled fish and vegetarian dishes served up on a quiet, sunny patio close to the beach.

✚ Off map, west ✉ 429 Ocean Front Walk, Venice Beach
☎ 310/392–4937 🚌 33

GORDON BIERSCH BREWERY (££)

Alfresco dining and people-watching, beers made on the premises and good California cuisine.

✚ Off map, northeast ✉ 41 Hugus Alley, Old Town Pasadena
☎ 626/449–0052 🚌 177

GREENBLATT'S (£)

A haven for homesick New Yorkers, with deli favourites from corned beef to cheesecake.

✚ B2 ✉ 8017 Sunset Boulevard, West Hollywood
☎ 323/656–0606 🚌 2

INN OF THE 7TH RAY (££)

Laid-back New Age hangout in lovely setting. Vegetarian and organic menu plus special barbecued chicken.

✚ Off map, west ✉ 128 Old Topanga Road, Malibu
☎ 310/455–1311

ROCKENWAGNER (££)

European ambience and beautifully prepared dishes using the freshest local ingredients.

✚ Off map, west ✉ 2435 Main Street, Santa Monica
☎ 310/399–6504
◷ Brunch Sat, Sun; dinner daily 🚌 33, SM1

VERSAILLES (£)

A taste of Havana in Southern Cal serving great value large portions.

✚ Off map, west
✉ 10319 Venice Boulevard
☎ 310/558–3168 🚌 33

Eating with children

LA's chic dining haunts are not particularly child friendly, but family restaurants and burger chains abound, particularly near Disneyland and around South Bay, and children love perching at the bar at one of the 1950s-style themed diners to slurp on a milkshake or munch fries. Always check if the restaurant has a children's menu and crayons and paper on hand – or bring your own.

CAFÉS & COFFEE SHOPS

Rocketing back in time

If you really get into the retro thing on Melrose Avenue, Johnny Rocket's, 7507 Melrose (corner of Gardner), West Hollywood, is the ultimate 1950s-style diner where you can order up a milkshake to match your new second-hand poodle skirt or strike a suitably Jimmy Dean pose over a hamburger and monopolise the juke box. And for something completely different, don't miss the wonderfully wacky flower petal-look street lamps diagonally across the street.

Sunday brunch

When Sunday rolls around, Angeleonos gear up to 'do' brunch, which is generally served from around 10 or 11 until 2. Numerous restaurants throughout the city lay on a variation of the combination breakfast and lunch theme with a set-price menu. However, the most popular brunch spots tend to be found on the coast, and patio dining is at a premium.

CROCODILE CAFÉ (£)
One of a fast-growing chain of informal, California cuisine cafés with gourmet pizzas, pasta and salads.
➕ Off map, west ✉ 101 Santa Monica Boulevard, Santa Monica ☎ 310/394–4783 🚌 21, 22, 33, SM1, 7, 10

ED DEBEVIC'S (££)
1950s theme diner with wacky waitresses, burgers, chilli and calorific pies.
➕ Off map, west ✉ 134 N La Cienega Boulevard, Beverly Hills ☎ 310/659–1952 🚌 20, 21, 22, 105

MARKET CITY CAFFE (££)
Nibble on pizza, salads, and antipasto on the outdoor patio, plus a glass of chilled white California vino.
➕ Off map, northeast ✉ 33 S Fair Oaks Avenue, Old Town Pasadena ☎ 626/568–0203 🕐 Brunch Sun; lunch, dinner daily 🚌 212

ORIGINAL PANTRY CAFÉ (£)
Owned by ex-mayor Riordan, this no-nonsense spot serves hearty food on wood tables.
➕ L8 ✉ 8775 Figueroa Street, Downtown ☎ 213/972–9279 🚌 81

PATINETTE AT MOCA (£-££)
Acclaimed chef Joachim Splichal created the café's menu with many original options. Located in the Museum of Contemporary Art.
➕ M7 ✉ 250 S Grand Avenue ☎ 213/626–1178 🚌 DASH B

SIDEWALK CAFÉ (£)
Great people-watching from the beachfront terrace. Sandwiches, salads, tostadas, burgers.
➕ Off map, west ✉ 1401 Ocean Front Walk, Venice Beach ☎ 310/399–5547 🚌 33

ROSE CAFÉ (£-££)
Outdoor seating, tempting baked good and out-of-work actors, plus soothing ocean breezes.
➕ Off map, west ✉ 220 Rose Avenue, Santa Monica ☎ 213/656–6388 🚌 SM1, 8, 10

VILLAGE COFFEE SHOP (£)
Laid-back, friendly haunt of creative types in the Hollywood Hills; good home-cooked food.
➕ Off map, northwest ✉ 2695 N Beachwood Drive, Hollywood ☎ 323/467–5398 🕐 Mon–Sat 🚌 208

WOLFGANG PUCK CAFÉ (£)
Sample abbreviated versions of the master's California-Asian fusion fare. Also Santa Monica and Universal City.
➕ B2 ✉ 8000 Sunset Boulevard, West Hollywood ☎ 323/650–7300 🚌 2, 3

WORLD CAFÉ (£-££)
Busy restaurant/bar with a good line in wood-fired pizzas, pastas and vegetarian dishes.
➕ Off map, west ✉ 2820 Main Street, Santa Monica ☎ 310/392–1661 🚌 33, SM1

GRAB AN INEXPENSIVE BITE TO EAT

APPLE PAN (£)

An LA institution with 1950s counter seating, messy hickory burgers and scrumptious apple and berry pies. Always popular at lunchtimes.
🕇 Off map, west ✉ 10801 W Pico Boulevard, W LA ☎ 310/475–3585 🚌 212

BELMONT BREWING COMPANY (£–££)

Home-brewed beer and casual American menu. Dine out on the beachfront terrace.
🕇 Off map, south ✉ 25 39th Place, Long Beach ☎ 562/433–3891 🚌 LBT 121

CANTER'S (£)

Classic Fairfax District deli serving kosher specials, huge pastrami sandwiches, home-made pickles and waitress banter 24 hours a day.
🕇 B4 ✉ 419 N Fairfax Avenue Midtown ☎ 323/651–2030 🚌 14, 217

CHIN CHIN (£)

No additives allowed at this healthy Chinese LA chain famous for its Chinese chicken salda, low-fat alternatives and chocolate-covered fortune cookies. Other outposts in Brentwood, Marina del Rey and Studio City.
🕇 Off map, west ✉ 8618 Sunset Boulevard, West Hollywood ☎ 310/652–1818 🚌 2, 3, 429

DUKE'S (£)

No-frills, entertainment industry hangout. Nothing over $10.
🕇 Off map, west ✉ 8909 Sunset Boulevard, West Hollywood ☎ 310/652–3100 🚌 2, 3

KOKOMO (£)

Freshly baked muffins, deli sandwiches, steaming bowls of tasty gumbo, salads – all good reasons to brave the Farmer's Market.
🕇 B4 ✉ Farmer's Market, 6333 W 3rd Street, Midtown ☎ 323/933–0773 🚌 16, 217

LA BREA BAKERY (£)

Although this bakery is attached to a terrific Italian restaurant (Campanile), the thing to go for is brunch. Some of the best breads in the country come out of baker Nancy Silverton's ovens.
🕇 Off map, west ✉ 624 S La Brea Avenue ☎ 213/938 1447 🕐 Brunch Sat, Sun; lunch, dinner daily 🚌 212

MANDARIN DELI (£)

Chinese dim sum and noodle dishes every which way.
🕇 N6 ✉ 727 N Broadway ☎ 213/623–6054 🚌 DASH B

PHILIPPE THE ORIGINAL (£)

Crusty fried bread, French dip sandwiches piled high with meats, cheese and extra hot mustard. Heroic breakfasts, homemade pies.
🕇 N6 ✉ 1001 N Alameda Street ☎ 213/628–3781 🚇 Union Station 🚌 DASH B

PINK'S FAMOUS CHILI DOGS (£)

This take-away stand serves foot-long jalepeño dogs, burgers and tamales until 2AM.
🕇 C3 ✉ 709 N La Brea ☎ 323/931–4223 🚌 212

Malls and markets

LA's numerous shopping malls, such as the Beverly Center (► 71) and Downtown's Seventh Marketplace (► 71), are a good source of cheap eats offering a wide choice of fast-food outlets as well as delis and ethnic take-away counters with shared seating. The touristy-tacky Farmer's Market (► 71) offers everything from delectable doughnuts to fresh produce and is particularly popular at weekends, while the down-to-earth Grand Central Market (► 38) is the best place to find budget bites Downtown bar none.

Home delivery

Call 800–PINK-DOT for a 30-minute home delivery of everything from groceries or video rentals to pizza or prophylactics. A S3 charge is added to each order. There are locations in West Hollywood, Westwood and the South Bay. Call for a complete catalogue.

SHOPPING DISTRICTS

MAIN STREET

Hip boutiques, arty design and novelty shops helpfully interspersed with good restaurants.

⊕ Off map, west ✉ Main Street (between Hollister and Rose avenues), Santa Monica 🚌 SM1, 8, 10

MELROSE AVENUE

A 3-mile strip of the esoteric and exotic from cutting-edge fashion and retro boutiques to galleries and gift shops. Riveting window-shopping, dining and entertainment.

⊕ D3 ✉ Melrose Avenue (between Highland Avenue and Doheny Drive), Hollywood 🚌 10, 11

The Garment District

Downtown's Garment District is a great spot for bargain hunters. Centred around Los Angeles Street (between 8th and 11th streets), it offers dozens of discount retail, jobber and manufacturers' outlet shops with fashion buys at bargain prices. Check out the Cooper Building, one of Southern California's largest outlet and discount fashion centres, at 860 Los Angeles Street, with more than 50 shops spread over six floors.

MONTANA AVENUE

Ten blocks of super up-scale shopping, designer boutiques, elegant home-decorating emporiums, antique shops and luxurious beauty salons for the woman with almost everything.

⊕ Off map, west ✉ Montana Avenue (between 7th and 17th streets), Santa Monica 🚌 SM3, 9

OLD TOWN PASADENA

Bisected by Colorado Boulevard, this attractively restored 12-square block enclave offers an appealing selection of boutiques galleries, gift shops and eateries.

⊕ Off map, northeast ✉ Colorado Boulevard (between Arroyo Parkway and Delacey Avenue), Pasadena 🚌 177, 180, 181, 401, 402, 483, 485

RODEO DRIVE

LA's answer to London's Bond Street and Rome's Via Condotti, Rodeo Drive is a gold-plated shopping experience. Top designer clothes and accessories, a surfeit of jewellers and chic retail complexes.

⊕ Off map, west ✉ Rodeo Drive, Beverly Hills 🚌 4, 20, 21, 22

SUNSET PLAZA

An exclusive little cluster of ultra-fashionable boutiques and pavement bistros on 'The Strip'.

⊕ Off map, west ✉ Sunset Boulevard (between San Vicente and La Cienega boulevards), West Hollywood 🚌 2, 3

THIRD STREET PROMENADE

Shoppers, street musicians and street vendors jostle along the pedestrianised Promenade with many shopping, dining and entertainment options.

⊕ Off map, west ✉ 3rd Street (between Wilshire Boulevard and Broadway), Santa Monica 🚌 4, 20, 22, SM1, 2, 3, 7, 8, 9, 10

WESTWOOD VILLAGE

Mediterranean-style village whose fashion, cinemas and music stores appeal to students from the neighbouring UCLA campus (▶ 18). Many cafés.

⊕ Off map, west ✉ Westwood Boulevard (off Wilshire Boulevard), Westwood 🚌 20, 21, 22, SM1, 2, 3, 8, 12

SHOPPING CENTRES & MALLS

BEVERLY CENTER

Major league mall with more than 160 upscale fashion, department and speciality shops and cinemas and restaurants.
➕ Off map, west ✉ 8500 Beverly Boulevard, West Hollywood ☎ 310/854–0070
🚌 14, 16, 105, 220

CENTURY CITY SHOPPING CENTER & MARKETPLACE

LA's premier outdoor shopping, dining and entertainment complex, with some 140 shops.
➕ Off map, west ✉ 10250 Santa Monica Boulevard, West LA
☎ 310/277–3898
🚌 4, 22, 322

DEL AMO FASHION CENTER

Humongous South Bay retail centre with more than 300 shops, ten anchor stores, dining and cinemas.
➕ Off map, southwest ✉ Hawthorne Boulevard (at Carson), Torrance
☎ 310/542–8525

FOX HILLS MALL

Locataed near LAX airport in Culver City, this shopping centre boasts 140 shops.
➕ Off map, southeast ✉ 200 Fox Hills Mall, Culver City
☎ 310/390–7833 🚌 234

GLENDALE GALLERIA

Giant San Gabriel Valley mall featuring Macy's, Nordstrom and J C Penney with some 250 other shops and restaurants.
➕ Off map, north ✉ 2148 Glendale Galleria, Glendale
☎ 818/240–9481
🚌 180, 181

SANTA MONICA PLACE

Three storeys of boutiques, accessories, kids' clothes, lingerie from Frederick's of Hollywood, Williams-Sonoma cookshop, plus a food court.
➕ Off map, west ✉ Broadway at 3rd Street, Santa Monica
☎ 310/394–5451 🚌 4, 20, 22, 33, SM1, 2, 3, 7, 8, 9, 10

SEVENTH MARKETPLACE

Relatively modest open-air Downtown mall with a brace of department stores and a food court.
➕ L7 ✉ 735 S Figueroa Street ☎ 213/955–7150
🚌 DASH A, E, F

SOUTH COAST PLAZA

Massive, hugely successful Orange County mall. US department stores, European designers, kids' entertainment.
➕ Off map, southeast ✉ 3333 Bristol Street, Costa Mesa ☎ 714/435–2000

UNIVERSAL CITYWALK

Eclectic gifts, souvenirs and entertainment outside Universal Studios.
➕ Off map, northwest ✉ 1000 Universal Center Drive, Universal City ☎ 818/622–4455 🚌 420, 424, 425

WESTSIDE PAVILION

Chic selection of men's and women's fashions, gifts, dining and cinema.
➕ Off map, west ✉ 10800 W Pico Boulevard, West LA ☎ 310/474–6255 🚌 SM7, 8, 12, 13

Farmer's Market

Born in the 1930s Depression, at 6333 W 3rd Street, Midtown, when local farmers would bring their produce here in search of buyers, the market has metamorphosed into an LA institution. It's touristy, and tacky souvenirs abound, but you can still find fresh fruit and vegetables, butchers, bakers, deli counters and great value fast food from coffee and doughnuts to po'boy sandwiches.

MEN'S & WOMEN'S CLOTHING

'Department Store Row'

As if Rodeo Drive were not enough to keep Beverly Hills' gold card-toting matrons occupied between lunches, LA's 'Department Store Row' lies a mere stretch limo's length away. Neiman Marcus (✉ 9700 Wilshire Boulevard ☎ 310/550–5900), Saks Fifth Avenue (✉ 9600 Wilshire Boulevard ☎ 310/275–4211), and Barneys New York (✉ 9570 Wilshire Boulevard ☎ 310/276–4400) offer the full complement of fashions, furnishings, gifts and cosmetics.

THE COCKPIT

Packed floor to ceiling with Americana from leather flying jackets, jeans and baseball caps to Harley Davidson bike boots, badges and collectables.

✚ A3 ✉ 7510 Melrose Avenue, West Hollywood ☎ 323/782–0617 🚌 10, 11

DREAM DRESSER

Latex, leather and downright lascivious gear created with dream weavers and exotic clubbers in mind.

✚ Off map, west ✉ 8444–50 Santa Monica Boulevard, West Hollywood ☎ 323/848–3480 🚌 4

GIORGIO BEVERLY HILLS

Veteran Rodeo Drive designer and perfumier. Ladies-who-lunch, charming staff and outrageous prices.

✚ Off map, west ✉ 327 N Rodeo Drive, Beverly Hills ☎ 310/274–0200 🚌 20, 21 22

GUESS?

Fashionable and comfortable suits and casual clothing for men and women, plus great kidswear at several locations around town. Also outlet bargains in the Cooper Building (▶ 70, panel).

✚ Off map, west ✉ Unit 3, Century City Shopping Center, West LA ☎ 310/556–0123 🚌 4

JAY WOLF

Tucked away in a small courtyard, Wolf specialises in discreet and comfortable modern designer clothing (Paul Smith, Hugo Boss) for men and women.

✚ Off map, west ✉ 517 N Robertson Boulevard, West Hollywood ☎ 310/273–9893 🚌 10, 11, 220

MAXFIELD'S

Designer fashions for men and women, plus furniture, antiques, jewellery and housewares.

✚ Off map, west ✉ 8825 Melrose Avenue, West Hollywood ☎ 310/274–8800 🚌 10. 11, 220

RON HERMAN FRED SEGAL

Legendary and eternally hip Melrose speciality store complex. Sportswear and designer collections for men, women and children, gifts, accessories, lingerie and luggage.

✚ A3 ✉ 8100 Melrose Avenue, West Hollywood ☎ 323/651–4129 🚌 10, 11

TOMMY HILFIGER

Hilfiger has captured the LA celebrity crowd with a funky and glittery, Rock 'N' Roll collection for pop and rock stars.

✚ Off map, west ✉ 468 N Rodeo Drive, Beverly Hills ☎ 310/888–0132 🚌 4

VIN BAKER

Stylish sandals, adorable purses and high-end women's clothing at this shop, perched on a fashionable stretch of La Brea. A second location in Santa Monica.

✚ C4 ✉ 132 S La Brea Avenue, Midtown ☎ 323/936–4001 🚌 14, 212

RETRO & SECOND-HAND CLOTHING

AARDVARKS
Barnlike vintage clothing store. Dinner jackets from bandleader-flash to butler's tails, frocks and feather boas, accessories and wig bin. Also in Pasadena and Venice.
✚ B3 ✉ 7579 Melrose Avenue, West Hollywood ☎ 323/655–6769 🚌 10, 11

AMERICAN RAG
Vast second-hand clothes and accessories emporium. Tuxes, grunge, ex-military great coats, 1970s glam and 1980s unspeakable.
✚ Off map, west ✉ 150 S La Brea, Midtown ☎ 323/935–3154 🚌 14, 212, 316

AMERICAN VINTAGE
The 'worn-out-West' look – previously loved denim, *Top Gun* aviator jackets, bowling shirts, aloha prints, plus US collectables, vintage Zippos and Native American jewellery.
✚ C3 ✉ 645 N Martel Avenue, West Hollywood ☎ 323/653–5645 🚌 10, 11

GOTTA HAVE IT
Behind an eye-catching playing card design façade, serried ranks of wildly assorted retro wear for guys and gals.
✚ Off map, west ✉ 1516 Pacific Avenue, Venice Beach ☎ 310/392–5949 🚌 SM7

IT'S A WRAP
Movie and television studio wardrobe departments offload their extravagances at this bulging Valley store.
✚ Off map, north ✉ 3315 W Magnolia Boulevard, Burbank ☎ 818/567–7366 🚌 183

PAPER BAG PRINCESS
One-of-a-kind vintage designer dresses and accessories from the likes of Alaïa, Yves St-Laurent and Maud Frizon.
✚ Off map, west ✉ 8700 Santa Monica Boulevard, West Hollywood ☎ 310/358–1985 🚌 4

PARIS 1900
Antique garments and linens. Original Victorian and Edwardian collector's pieces for very special occasions. Open by appointment or by chance.
✚ Off map, west ✉ 2703 Main Street, Santa Monica ☎ 310/396–0405 🚌 33, SM1

REEL CLOTHES AND PROPS
Thrift-shopping with a difference: all these cast-offs have a glittering pedigree. This is the place to pick up slinky frocks and other nearly new items culled from the closets of studio wardrobe departments.
✚ Off map, west ✉ 12132 Ventura Boulevard, Studio City ☎ 818/508–7762 🚌 424, 425, 522, 218

WASTELAND
Unmissable metal and mosaic façade fronting a funky collection of velvet, vinyl and lurex delights, fluffy angora tops and leopard-print hotpants.
✚ C3 ✉ 7428 Melrose Avenue, West Hollywood ☎ 213/653–3028 🚌 10, 11

More designers, more vintage

Both La Brea Avenue and Robertston Boulevard have established themselves as speciality shopping destinations for LA's myriad shopaholics in search of that perfect outfit. The stretch of Robertson between Wilshire and Beverly boulevards boasts outposts for the designers such as Cynthia Rawley and Kate Spade. La Brea, between Santa Monica and Wilshire, draws pedestrian traffic and sells everything from vintage to designer ware to antiques.

ANTIQUES & ART

Mission West

South Pasadena's turn-of-the-century Mission West shopping district is a favourite haunt for antique browsing. Along pretty, tree-shaded Mission Street there are more than half-a-dozen antiques dealers including furniture and collectables at Mission Antiques ✉ 1018 Mission ☎ 626/799–1327 Yoko Japanese Antiques ✉ 1011 Mission ☎ 626/441–4758 and linen and bric-a-brac at Hodgson's Antiques ✉ 1007 Mission ☎ 626/799–0229

ANTIQUARIUS

A great place for a browse: more than 30 shops specialising in antique jewellery, silver, art glass and curios.
✚ Off map, west ✉ 8840 Beverly Boulevard, West Hollywood ☎ 310/274–2363 🚌 14

BERGAMOT STATION

This old trolley station now houses some 21 contemporary galleries dealing in an exciting range of art, sculpture, furniture, glass and photography.
✚ Off map, west ✉ 2525 Michigan Avenue, Santa Monica ☎ 310/829–5854 🚌 SM9

BROADWAY GALLERY COMPLEX

Another Santa Monica arts enclave specialising in contemporary paintings, prints and functional art such as furnishings with a distinctive California style.
✚ Off map, west ✉ 2018–2114 Broadway (between 20th & Cloverfield), Santa Monica 🚌 4, SM1, 10

ESTATE SALES & ANTIQUES

An elegant array of fine antique furniture and *objets d'art* including silver, glass, porcelain and jewellery.
✚ Off map, north ✉ 1012B Mission Street, Pasadena ☎ 626/799–8858 🚌 188, 256, 483

GEMINI G.E.L.

Prints by top American/US-based 20th-century artists including Rauschenberg, Jasper Johns, Hockney and Richard Diebenkorn.
✚ Off map, west ✉ 8365 Melrose Avenue, West Hollywood ☎ 323/651–0513 🚌 10, 11

LOUIS STERN FINE ARTS

Well-respected gallery specialising in Impressionist, Latin American, 20th-century and contemporary work.
✚ Off map, west ✉ 9002 Melrose Avenue, West Hollywood ☎ 310/276–0147 🚌 10, 11

MARGO LEAVIN GALLERY

Photography, paintings, sculpture and works on paper at this cutting-edge contemporary art gallery.
✚ Off map, west ✉ 812 N Robertson Boulevard, West Hollywood ☎ 310/273–0603 🚌 4, 220

SANTA MONICA ANTIQUE MARKET

120 stalls of antiques and collectables from around the world. Silver, jewellery, books, crockery, clothing, etc.
✚ Off map, west ✉ 1607 Lincoln Boulevard, Santa Monica ☎ 310/314–4899 🚌 SM3

SANTA MONICA TRADING COMPANY

Teetering piles of vintage magazines, second-hand books, film posters and appealing antique prints of fruit, fish and flowers are crammed into this intriguing small shop.
✚ Off map, west ✉ 2705 Main Street, Santa Monica ☎ 310/392–4806 🚌 33, SM1

BOOKS & MUSIC

A DIFFERENT LIGHT
A huge selection of gay and lesbian literature. Evening readings; a good place for free listings magazines.
➕ Off map, west ✉ 8853 Santa Monica Boulevard, West Hollywood ☎ 310/854–6601
🚌 4, 304

ACRES OF BOOKS
Rambling treasure trove of second-hand tomes on a host of topics.
➕ Off map, south ✉ 240 Long Beach Boulevard, Long Beach
☎ 562/437–6980 🚇 Metro Blue Line/Long Beach Boulevard

BARNES & NOBLE
Standout among LaLaLand B&Ns; encyclopedic selection and bestseller discounts.
➕ Off map, west ✉ 1201 3rd Street, Santa Monica
☎ 310/260–9110 🚌 4, 20, 22, SM1, 2, 3, 7, 8, 9, 10

BODHI TREE
New Age book shop where Shirley MacLaine got metaphysical.
➕ Off map, west ✉ 8585 Melrose Avenue, West Hollywood
☎ 310/659–1733 🚌 10, 11

BOOK SOUP
This voluminous book shop and newsstand has spawned a fashionable bistro next door. Classics to crime, reference books and more; art history and movie sections are good.
➕ Off map, west ✉ 8818 Sunset Boulevard, West Hollywood ☎ 310/659–3110
🚌 2, 3, 302, 429

BORDERS BOOKS AND MUSIC
An impressive selection of classic and contemporary literature and sounds, plus a handy in-store café.
➕ Off map, west ✉ 1415 3rd Street Promenade, Santa Monica
☎ 310/393–9290 🚌 4, 20, 21, 22, SM1, 2, 3, 7, 8, 9, 10

HEAR MUSIC
Small but inviting and user-friendly music shop with well-chosen rock, jazz, classical, folk and world music.
➕ Off map, west ✉ 1429 3rd Street Promenade, Santa Monica
☎ 310/319–9527 🚌 4, 20, 22, SM1, 2, 3, 7, 8, 9, 10

THE MYSTERIOUS BOOKSHOP
A gripping source of thrilling tomes.
➕ Off map, west ✉ 8763 Beverly Boulevard, West Hollywood ☎ 310/659–2959
🚌 14

SMALL WORLD BOOKS & THE MYSTERY ANNEXE
Convenient beachfront emporium: everything from classics and a few foreign language books to beach vacation mysteries, sex 'n' sun 'n' shopping sagas.
➕ Off map, west ✉ 1407 Ocean Front Walk, Venice Beach ☎ 310/399–2360 🚌 33

VIRGIN MEGASTORE
Like rival Tower Records (8801 Sunset) Richard Branson's Megastore encompasses the musical spectrum from obscure indie labels to Elgar.
➕ A2 ✉ 8000 Sunset Boulevard, West Hollywood
☎ 323/650–8666 🚌 2, 3, 302, 429

Whale of a design district

The interior design capital of the Pacific Rim, West Hollywood boasts a wealth of art and antiques galleries, plus around 300 speciality design shops and showrooms centred on the west end of Melrose Avenue and San Vicente boulevards. One unmissable sight here is Pacific Design Center (aka 'The Blue Whale' for its size and colour ► 55), which harbours more than 200 decorator showrooms offering furniture, fabrics, floor and wall coverings, lighting and kitchen products. The showrooms are now open to the general public (Mon–Fri 9–5), though some may require an appointment and others are open 'to the trade only'; still others have a designer on call to make the necessary referral.

MOVIE MEMORABILIA & SOUVENIRS

Ocean Front Walk

Looking for LA T-shirts, Dodgers Baseball caps, postcards and other souvenir tat? Then make a beeline for Venice Beach's open-air bazaar where the stalls are piled high with cheap LA-themed goods, $5 sunglasses, microscopic bikinis, West Coast thrash CDs and New Age tie-dye creations.

CHIC-A-BOOM
Huge selection of film and advertising posters, plus vintage magazines, TV and rock memorabilia including autographs, books, fanzines, photographs and posters.
➕ D3 ✉ 6817 Melrose Avenue, West Hollywood
☎ 323/931–7441 🚌 10, 11

CINEMA COLLECTORS
Mountains of memorabilia for the terminally star-struck. Lots of posters and photographs.
➕ E2 ✉ 1507 Wilcox Avenue, Hollywood ☎ 323/461–6516
🚌 1, 217

COLLECTORS' BOOKSTORE
The 'most comprehensive array of cinematic collectables on the planet' – apparently – movie stills, posters, magazines, scripts.
➕ E1 ✉ 6225 Hollywood Boulevard ☎ 323/467–3296
🚌 1, 217

THE DISNEY STORE
Goofy, Donald, Mickey and Minnie are joined by the Little Mermaid, the Lion King and other newcomers in the great merchandise heist.
➕ Off map, west ✉ Unit 39, Century City Shopping Center, 10250 Santa Monica Boulevard, West LA ☎ 310/556–8035
🚌 4, 304

FANTASIES COME TRUE
Nearly-new and antique Disney collectables from famous character toys and china figurines to buttons and posters.
➕ B3 ✉ 8012 Melrose Avenue, West Hollywood
☎ 323/655–2636 🚌 10, 11

LARRY EDMUNDS' BOOK SHOP
A small but rich trawling ground for cinematic bibliophiles stocking all sorts of film and theatre-related tomes, plus posters and stills.
➕ D1 ✉ 6644 Hollywood Boulevard, Hollywood
☎ 323/463–3273 🚌 1, 217

MOLETOWN
Current TV and movie knick-knacks include *Star Trek* monopoly, *Sopranos* mugs and *Friends* posters.
➕ C2 ✉ 900 N La Brea Avenue, West Hollywood
☎ 323/851–0111 🚌 212

SAMUEL FRENCH THEATER & FILM BOOKSHOP
For true aficionados and wannabe movie writers, this is the place to pick up specialist books and essential and obscure film and theatre scripts. Knowledgeable staff.
➕ B2 ✉ 7623 Sunset Boulevard, West Hollywood
☎ 323/876–0570 🚌 2, 3

WARNER BROTHERS STUDIO STORE
Bugs Bunny and the Loony Tunes crew feature on all manner of souvenir paraphernalia.
➕ Off map, west ✉ 270 Santa Monica Place (4th & Broadway), Santa Monica
☎ 310/393–6070 🚌 4, 33

SPECIALITY SHOPS & GIFTS

DEL MANO GALLERY
A terrific array of innovative and affordable contemporary crafts ranging from jewellery to art glass, ceramics and furnishings.
✚ Off map, northeast ✉ 33 E Colorado Boulevard, Pasadena
☎ 626/793–6648
🚊 180, 181

EVERY PICTURE TELLS A STORY
Captivating bookstore-gallery displaying original art and lithographs from children's books: Eric Carle, Tim Burton, Maurice Sendak.
✚ B4 ✉ 7525 Beverly Boulevard, Midtown
☎ 323/932–6070 🚊 14

LA EYEWORKS
From the town that never removes its shades, face furniture for every occasion.
✚ C3 ✉ 7407 Melrose Avenue, West Hollywood
☎ 323/653–8255 🚊 10, 11

MOE'S FLOWERS
Need to say it with flowers? This corner shop brims over with orchids, lilies, roses, exotic blooms and foliage.
✚ A3 ✉ 8101 Melrose Avenue, West Hollywood
☎ 323/653–5444 🚊 10, 11

MRS BEASLEY'S
Fudge brownies with powdered sugar, Miss Grace's lemon cake and macaroons are among the mouth-watering baked goods. Deliveries to order.
✚ Off map, west ✉ 255

Beverly Drive, Beverly Hills
☎ 800/710–7742
🚊 180, 181

PLASTICA
Woven bags, chopsticks, teapots, sandals, potato mashers and more – all made out of plastic.
✚ H1 ✉ 4685 Hollywood Boulevard ☎ 323/644–1212
🚊 26, 354

SOOLIP PAPERIE & PRESS
Amazing stationery shop: racks of colourful handmade papers, coloured inks, hip pens and desk accessories. Check out the Bungalow across the garden courtyard for its delectable range of silk pyjamas, sumptious bed covers and alluring bath products .
✚ Off map, west ✉ 8646 Melrose Avenue, West Hollywood
☎ 310/360–0545 🚊 10, 11

WANNA BUY A WATCH?
Vintage and contem-porary timepieces from Bulova to Betty Boop, Tiffany dress watches, US military issue, plus antique diamond and art-deco jewellery.
✚ C3 ✉ 7366 Melrose Avenue, West Hollywood
☎ 323/653–0467 🚊 10, 11

THE WOUND & WOUND TOY CO
A nostalgic array of windup cars, trains and trucks, plus robots, singing birthday cakes and Etch-A-Sketch keyrings.
✚ C3 ✉ 7374 Melrose Avenue, West Hollywood
☎ 323/653–6703 🚊 10, 11

St Elmo's Village
A hippy-funky alternative to the fashion victim chic on Melrose, this unlikely arts project in quiet suburbia – a group of old wooden bungalows with gardens full of cacti and sculpture – welcomes visitors at weekends. In the mural-covered courtyard, artists offer free workshops in sculpture, painting and drama from 10AM on Saturdays.
✉ 4830 St Elmo Drive (off South La Brea), Midtown
☎ 323/931–3409

CLASSICAL MUSIC & PERFORMING ARTS

Tickets

Concert and theatre tickets can be purchased direct through the venue, or through Ticketmaster (☎ 213/381–2000), which also supplies tickets to sporting events, and Ticket Time (☎ 310/473–1000).

Sightseeing concerts

Join the Da Camera Society (☎ 310/440–1351; membership not required) for an evening of chamber music in one of several intimate and historic sites around the city. The 'Chamber Music in Historic Sites' series has visited the Biltmore Hotel, the Huntington Library and also the *Queen Mary* among others.

BECKMAN AUDITORIUM

Host to the excellent Cal Tech After Dark performing arts season, which features theatre, music, dance, comedy and lectures.

➕ Off map, northeast ✉ 332 S Michigan Avenue, Pasadena ☎ 626/395–4652 🚌 401

GEFFEN PLAYHOUSE

Neighbourhood theatre with a fine reputation, intimate enough to host one-man shows.

➕ Off map, west ✉ 10886 Le Conte Avenue, Westwood ☎ 310/208–5454 🚌 20, 21, 22, SM1, 2, 3, 8, 12

HOLLYWOOD BOWL

Much-loved outdoor venue for the Los Angeles Philharmonic Orchestra's Symphony Under the Stars series (Jun–Sep) and other alfresco performances.

➕ Off map, northwest ✉ 2301 N Highland Avenue, Hollywood ☎ 323/850–2000 🚌 420

JAPAN AMERICA THEATER

Contemporary and traditional Japanese Noh plays and kabuki theatre.

➕ N7 ✉ 244 S San Pedro Street, Little Tokyo ☎ 213/680–3700 🚌 DASH A

MUSIC CENTER

LA's chief performing arts complex includes the Dorothy Chandler Pavilion (home to the LA Philharmonic's winter season), the Ahmanson Theatre (musicals, drama and comedy) and the Mark Taper Forum (drama and occasional music). It is also used by the Music Center Opera and the acclaimed Joffrey Ballet.

➕ M6 ✉ 135 N Grand Avenue ☎ 213/972–7211 🚇 Civic Center 🚌 DASH A, B

ODYSSEY THEATRE

One of the city's most highly regarded avant-garde theatre companies offers ensembles and visiting productions.

➕ Off map, west ✉ 2055 S Sepulveda Boulevard, West LA ☎ 310/477–2055 🚌 SM9

PASADENA CIVIC AUDITORIUM

Home of the Pasadena Symphony Orchestra, and a magnificent 1920s Moeller theatre organ. Also various theatre and dance events.

➕ Off map, northeast ✉ 300 E Green Street, Pasadena ☎ 626/449–7360 🚌 401

SHUBERT THEATER

Century City's saving grace if you happen to be a fan of lavish big-production musicals.

➕ Off map, west ✉ 2020 Avenue of the Stars, Century City, West LA ☎ 800/447–7400 🚌 4

UCLA CENTER FOR THE PERFORMING ARTS (WADSWORTH THEATER)

Off-campus facility offering more than 200 music and dance events a year from home-grown and visiting performers.

➕ Off map, west ✉ 10920 Wilshire Boulevard, Westwood ☎ 310/825–2101 🚌 20, 21, 22, SM2

ROCK, JAZZ & BLUES

THE BAKED POTATO
One of LA's best contemporary jazz spots. The stuffed baked potatoes aren't bad either.
✚ Off map, northwest
✉ 3787 Cahuenga Boulevard (at Lankershim), Studio City
☎ 818/980–1615 🚇 420

B B KING'S BLUES CLUB
Restaurant and club serving Delta-style food and live blues, occasionally from the master himself. Gospel brunch on Sundays.
✚ Off map, northwest
✉ Universal City Walk, Universal City ☎ 818/622–5464 🚇 420, 424, 425, 522

HOUSE OF BLUES
This tin-shack theme restaurant on Sunset attracts massive queues and a generous sprinkling of celebs for southern food and headline blues-rock acts.
✚ Off map, west ✉ 8430 Sunset Boulevard, West Hollywood ☎ 323/848–5100 🚇 2, 3

M BAR & GRILL
California bar and grill that supplements good food with nightly jazz, blues and alternative music sessions.
✚ Off map, south ✉ 213A Pine Avenue, Long Beach
☎ 562/435–2525 🚇 Blue Line/Pine Avenue 🚇 60

MCCABE'S GUITAR SHOP
Guitar store by day, R&B-rock-jazz-folk showcase on Friday and Saturday nights with some pretty impressive names. Intimate, informal, alcohol-free but tea and biscuits available during musical acts.
✚ Off map, west ✉ 3101 W Pico Boulevard, Santa Monica
☎ 310/828–4403, 310/828–4497 🚇 SM7

THE MINT
Longstanding small blues bar with a faithful following and great music and atmosphere.
✚ Off map, west ✉ 6010 W Pico Boulevard, Midtown
✉ 323/954–9630 🚇 30

THE ROXY
Small, steamy rock venue, showcasing major recording acts and new bands via a sound system that knocks your socks off.
✚ Off map, west ✉ 9009 Sunset Boulevard, West Hollywood ☎ 310/276–2222 🚇 2, 3

THE VIPER ROOM
Co-owned by Johnny Depp, the Viper draws cool crowds and big names. Jam and dance nights.
✚ Off map, west ✉ 8852 Sunset Boulevard, West Hollywood ☎ 310/358–1881 🚇 2, 3

WHISKY A GO GO
Though there is less 'Go-Go' these days, this Sunset Strip stalwart is still a haven for hard rockers.
✚ Off map, west ✉ 8901 Sunset Boulevard, West Hollywood ☎ 310/652–4202 🚇 2, 3

Opening times
Most music bars are open nightly from around 9PM until 2AM. Headline acts tend to go on after 11PM, when the clubs start to liven up. Clubs and music bars are often closed on Sunday and Monday nights. Call ahead.

NIGHTCLUBS

Club circuit

For the dedicated clubber with plenty of stamina and deep pockets, LA NightHawks (☎ 310/392–1500) can arrange a VIP night on the town. Limousine transport and no-hassle entry to a host of music, cabaret, dance and comedy clubs for a fun night out.

ARENA
Huge dance club in a former warehouse once used for storing ice. Features theme nights from house and hip-hop to Latino. Live bands and DJs (Thu–Sun).
➕ D3 ✉ 6655 Santa Monica Boulevard, Hollywood
☎ 323/462–0714 🚌 4, 420

CINEGRILL
Sleek art-deco interior and an eclectic cabaret running the gamut from jazz to comedy. Deservedly popular.
➕ D1 ✉ Hollywood Roosevelt Hotel, 7000 Hollywood Boulevard, Hollywood
☎ 323/466–7000 🚌 1

CRUSH BAR
Casual club with a retro heart that beats to the Motown and soul sound of 1960s and1970s. Great dancing; reggae and hip-hop nights.
➕ E2 ✉ 1735 N Cahuenga Boulevard, Hollywood
☎ 323/461–9017 🚌 1

FLORENTINE GARDENS
A dressy young clientele frequents this hip danceteria (Thu–Sun) with cool DJs and free buffet.
➕ F1 ✉ 5951 Hollywood Boulevard, Hollywood
☎ 323/464–0706 🚌 1, 217

THE GATE
Chic dinner-dance club with music ranging from techno to hip-hop. Outdoor patios and California cuisine.
➕ Off map, west ✉ 643 N La Cienega Boulevard, West Hollywood ☎ 310/289–8808
🚌 10, 11

LUNA PARK
Two stages in this sleek club showcase everything from pop to alternative to comedy. Go downstairs to the low-ceilinged cabaret or to the main room at the back. Dinner served; three bars.
➕ off map, west ✉ 665 N Robertson, West Hollywood
☎ 310/652–0611 🚌 4, 220

MAYAN
A fashionably dressy crowd swings to salsa and disco in an exotic former theatre Downtown.
➕ L8 ✉ 1038 S Hill Street
☎ 213/746–4287 🚌 DASH D

THE PALACE
Staggeringly loud sound system, two dance floors, four bars, opposite Capitol Records Building. Hip-hop, house, R&B and retro (Thu–Sat).
➕ E1 ✉ 1735 N Vine Street, Hollywood ☎ 323/467–4571
🚌 1, 217

THE PROBE
New wave, industrial, Brit pop and 1960s nights, plus a well-attended gay men's party on Saturdays.
➕ D3 ✉ 836 N Highland Avenue, Hollywood
☎ 323/460–6630 🚌 10, 11

RAGE
Packed West Hollywood gay club for boys serving Top 40, house, Latin and progressive, drag comedy and variety.
➕ Off map, west ✉ 8911 Santa Monica Boulevard, West Hollywood ☎ 310/652–7055
🚌 4, 304

BARS

BARNEY'S BEANERY
Convivial bar with pool tables and lengthy beer menu squeezed up against a Tex-Mex dining room (➤ 66).
✚ Off map, west ✉ 8447 Santa Monica Boulevard, West Hollywood ☎ 323/654–2287 🚌 4, 304

CASEY'S BAR & GRILL
Popular in the early evening with Downtown office workers. Happy hour and piano music.
✚ M7 ✉ 613 S Grand Avenue ☎ 213/629–2353 🚌 DASH B, C, E

CAT 'N' FIDDLE PUB
Lively young crowd comes to enjoy the outdoor patio, English beer on tap and visiting rock musicians.
✚ E2 ✉ 6530 Sunset Boulevard, Hollywood ☎ 323/468–3800 🚌 2, 3

CHEZ JAY
Laid-back neighbourhood beach bar with a broad clientele and a great juke box.
✚ Off map, west ✉ 1657 Ocean Avenue, Santa Monica ☎ 310/395–1741 🚌 20, 22, 33, SM1, 10

FOUR SEASONS
Celebrity-watching in a refined, relaxed hotel lounge setting.
✚ Off map, west ✉ 300S Doheny Drive, Beverly Hills ☎ 310/273–2222 🚌 16, 27

HARVELLE'S
Westside neighbourhood bar-cum-terrific blues club.
✚ Off map, west ✉ 1432 4th Street, Santa Monica ☎ 310/395–1676 🚌 4, SM1, 9, 10

MOLLY MALONE'S IRISH PUB
Venerable Irish-American institution. Guinness, darts and Irish music.
✚ Off map, west ✉ 575 S Fairfax Avenue (south of Melrose Avenue), Midtown ☎ 323/935–1577 🚌 10, 11, 217

MUSSO & FRANK
Hollywood's oldest and most celebrated bar and grill.
✚ D2 ✉ 6667 Hollywood Boulevard, Hollywood ☎ 323/467–7788 🚌 1, 217

SKY BAR
Glamorous Mondrian Hotel (➤ 84) poolside bar with fantastic city views. Open only to hotel guests and visitors with reservations.
✚ Off map, west ✉ 8440 Sunset Boulevard, West Hollywood ☎ 323/650–8999 🚌 2, 3, 302, 429

VODA
A post-work Manhattan-type crowd frequents this vodka bar in Santa Monica.
✚ Off map, west ✉ 1449 2nd Street, Santa Monica ☎ 310/394–9774 🚌 SM2, 4, 20, 22

YE OLDE KING'S HEAD
Popular with local Brits. Draft beer, darts, pub grub and heroic English breakfasts.
✚ Off map, west ✉ 116 Santa Monica Boulevard, Santa Monica ☎ 310/451–1402 🚌 4, 20, 22, 33, SM1 7, 10

The high life

Can't afford $350 a night for a swank hotel? Consider a martini at a hotel bar instead. Views and people-watching perks don't cost extra. In addition to Sky Bar and Four Seasons (see left), try one of the following:

the Regent Beverly Wilshire (✉ 9500 Wilshire Boulevard ☎ 310/275–5200)

Fenix at the Argyle (✉ 8358 Sunset Boulevard ☎ 323/848–6677)

Sunset Marquis' Whiskey Bar (✉ 1200 N Alta Loma Road ☎ 310/657–0611)

W Hotel (✉ 8930 Hilgard Avenue ☎ 310/208–8765).

OTHER AFTER-DARK IDEAS

Catch a movie

New-release Hollywood movies often hit the screens in LA before they turn up in other parts of the country. To catch the latest releases check what's on at the multi-screen Universal City 18 Cinemas (☎ 818/508–0588), or take a stroll around Westwood Village, where half-a-dozen theatres offer everything from first-run movies to the classics. One of the best repertory cinemas screening art-house and foreign-language offerings is the Nuart Theater (☎ 11272 Santa Monica Boulevard, at Sawtrelle Avenue, West LA ☎ 310/478–6379).

BOB'S BIG BOY
Serried ranks of LA's coolest customised hot rods wheel up at this Valley diner on a Friday night. It's the Petersen (➤ 29) for real.
✚ Off map, northwest
✉ 4211 Riverside Drive, Burbank ☎ 818/843–9334

COMEDY & MAGIC CLUB
Lively spot with stand-up comedy (occasional big names) spliced with magic acts.
✚ Off map, southwest
✉ 1018 Hermosa Avenue, Hermosa Beach
☎ 310/372–1193 ▣ 439

COMEDY STORE
Three stages showcase funsters who are up-and-coming, have made it or are just plain HUGE. One of the city's premier clubs.
✚ Off map, west ✉ 8433 Sunset Boulevard, West Hollywood ☎ 323/656–6225
▣ 2, 3

GRIFFITH PARK OBSERVATORY
Spectacular views of the city and no charge for stargazing through the Observatory's 12-inch telescope (➤ 33).
✚ Off map, northwest
✉ 2800 Observatory Road, Griffith Park
☎ 323/664–1181 ▣ 96

GROUNDLINGS THEATER
Talented improvisa-tional comedy troupe in short-run shows. Very popular – book ahead.
✚ C3 ✉ 7307 Melrose Avenue, West Hollywood
☎ 323/934–9700 ▣ 10, 11

HOLLYWOOD STAR LINES
Clean, wholesome fun at this bowling alley, knocking pins down while wearing used shoes.
✚ G3 ✉ 5227 Santa Monica Boulevard, Hollywood
☎ 323/665–4111 ▣ 4, 304

THE IMPROV
A popular new-material testing ground for big-name comics. Booking is recommended.
✚ A2 ✉ 8162 Melrose Avenue, West Hollywood
☎ 323/651–2583 ▣ 10, 11

JAZZ BAKERY
Housed in the beloved Helms Bakery building, Culver City's alcohol-free jazz spot welcomes patrons of all ages. Pastries and hot beverages are served.
✚ Off map, west ✉ 3233 Helms Avenue, Culver City
☎ 310/271–9039
▣ 33, 333

PASADENA POPS
Summer concerts in Descanso Gardens (➤ 57). Bring a picnic or order one with your ticket.
✚ Off map, northeast
✉ 1418 Descanso Drive, La Cañada ☎ 626/792–POPS

WIZARDZ
A nightclub featuring magicians, tarot card readers, fortune-tellers and dinner shows with laser displays.
✚ Off map, northwest
✉ CityWalk, Universal City
☎ 818/506–0066 ▣ 420

GYMS, SPAS & SPORTS

AIDA THIBIANT EUROPEAN DAY SPA

A rollcall of Hollywood's most glamorous female movie stars come here for massage, facials, manicures, makeup and skin treatments.
✚ Off map, west ✉ 449 N Cañon Drive, Beverly Hills ☎ 310/278–7565 🚊 3, 4, 304

BALLY TOTAL FITNESS

Chain of health clubs. Facilities may include fully equipped weight rooms, pools and squash courts, aerobics classes and spa treatments. Call for locations.
☎ 800/846–0256

BURKE WILLIAMS DAY SPA & MASSAGE CENTER

Celebrity favourite for hedonistic beauty treatments from facials and pedicures to thermal seaweed wraps.
✚ Off map, west ✉ 1460 4th Street, Santa Monica ☎ 310/587–3366 🚊 4, 22

GOLD'S GYM

Home of the Gold's Gym world-wide body-building empire.
✚ Off map, west ✉ 360 Hampton Drive, Venice Beach ☎ 310/392–6004 🚊 33, SM1

GRIFFITH PARK GOLF

Two 18-hole and two 9-hole courses. Facilities include club rental, carts, proshop, dining and night-lit driving range.
✚ Off map, northwest ✉ Griffith Park Drive, Griffith Park ☎ Information and reservations 323/663–2555 🚊 96

GRIFFITH PARK TENNIS

More than two dozen courts (available both day and night) at three locations. Reservations required but chance callers accepted space permitting.
✚ Off map, northwest ✉ Griffith Park Drive and Vermont Canyon, Griffith Park ☎ Information and reservations 323/664–3521, 323/661–5318 🚊 96

SANTA ANITA RACE TRACK

A lovely track in the shadow of the San Gabriel Mountains. Thoroughbred horse-racing December to April, October and November. Free viewing of morning workouts and weekend tram tours.
✚ Off map, northeast ✉ 285 W Huntington Drive, Arcadia ☎ 626/574–7223 🚊 79, 187, 188, 379

WORLD GYM

Another legendary workout facility (rivaling Gold's) for the Nautilus narcissists. Other locations in Pasadena and Burbank.
✚ Off map, west ✉ 3205 Washington Boulevard, Marina del Rey ☎ 310/827–8019 🚊 65

YOGA WORKS

Run into your favourite celeb as you assume the cobra pose at this Santa Monica studio.
✚ Off map, west ✉ 2nd floor 1426 Montana Avenue, Santa Monica ☎ 310/393–5150 🚊 SM3

Jogging

LA's most attractive option is probably the 22-mile beach path running south from Santa Monica. Or try Exposition Park downtown; Griffith Park in the Hollywood Hills; and, just to the west, the great trail around quiet Lake Hollywood, reached by car off Cahuenga Boulevard (via Dix Street).

Spectator sports

Catch the LA Dodgers (baseball) (☎ 323/224–1448) at home at the Dodger Stadium, north of Downtown. The LA Lakers (basketball) (☎ 213/742–7400), the LA Clippers (basketball) (☎ 213/742–7500), and the LA Kings (ice hockey) (☎ 888/546–4752) play at the Downtown Staples Center.

LUXURY HOTELS

Prices

The following price categories are per night based on two adults sharing a standard room, not including LA's 14 per cent transient occupancy tax:

Luxury hotels   over $200
Mid-range hotels $100 to $200
Budget hotels   up to $100

Per person:

Hostels $16–$23

Most hotels offer accommodation in several price ranges. If you are on a budget and the rate offered is at the top end of your limit, check to see if there is anything cheaper. Breakfast is not usually included. There is usually a parking fee at most hotels, which is as low as $5 at cheaper hotels and anywhere from $15–$23 at the luxury hotels. You may find package deals apply to hotels near Disneyland.

Cool off

Pools are generally found in luxury and mid-range hotels but not usually in the budget range.

BEVERLY HILLS HOTEL
Legendary pink palace on 12 landscaped and palm-fringed acres.
🚹 Off map, west ✉ 9641 Sunset Boulevard, Beverly Hills ☎ 310/276–2251 or 800/283–8885, fax 310/887–2887 🍴 Two restaurants, coffee shop, poolside café 🚌 2

CHATEAU MARMONT
Castle-style 1927 favourite of Gable, Lombard, Harlow et al; John Belushi died here.
🚹 A2 ✉ 8221 Sunset Boulevard, Hollywood ☎ 323/656–1010, or 800/242–8328, fax 323/655–5311 🍴 Dining room with fine wine cellar 🚌 2

HOTEL BEL-AIR
LA's most romantic hotel tucked away in a wooded canyon.
🚹 Off map, northwest ✉ 701 Stone Canyon Road, Bel-Air ☎ 310/472–1211, or 800/648–4097, fax 310/476–5890 🍴 Fine restaurant

LOS ANGELES DOWNTOWN MARRIOT
Fine Downtown hotel with oversize rooms, wall-to-wall windows, and superb city views.
🚹 M7 ✉ 333 S Figueroa Street ☎ 3213/617–1133, or 800/228–9290, fax 213/613–0291 🍴 Very good restaurant and grill 🚌 DASH A

MONDRIAN
Ultra-chic Ian Schrager/ Philippe Starck co-production. Large rooms with scented candles, CDs, orchids and city views.
🚹 Off map, west ✉ 8440 Sunset Boulevard ☎ 323/650–8999, or 800/525 8029, fax 323/650–5215 🍴 Restaurant, Sky Bar (► 81) 🚌 2, 3, 302

NEW OTANI
Luxury in little Tokyo. Rooms have Western beds or Japanese futons. No pool.
🚹 N7 ✉ 120 S Los Angeles Street ☎ 213/629–1200, or 800/421–8795, fax 213/622–0980 🍴 Three restaurants, Thousand Cranes (► 65) 🚌 DASH A

REGENT BEVERLY WILSHIRE
275 rooms in this sumptuous European-style grand hotel.
🚹 Off map, west ✉ 9500 Wilshire Boulevard, Beverly Hills ☎ 310/275–5200, or 800/427–4354, fax 310/274–2851 🍴 Excellent restaurant, The Dining Room (► 64) 🚌 20, 21, 22

RITZ-CARLTON HUNTINGTON
Beautifully restored 1907 hotel; luxurious facilities, stunning gardens.
🚹 Off map, northeast ✉ 1401 S Oak Knoll, Pasadena ☎ 626/568–3900, or 800/241–3333, fax 626/568–3700 🍴 Famous grill room

SHUTTERS ON THE BEACH
Lovely rooms and suites in a New England-style inn right on the beach.
🚹 Off map, west ✉ One Pico Boulevard, Santa Monica ☎ 310/458–0030, or 800/334–9000, fax 310/458–4589 🍴 Very good restaurant 🚌 22, 33

MID-RANGE HOTELS

CARLYLE INN

Delightful small hotel with spa, fitness centre, free local shuttle and complimentary breakfast buffet. No pool.

✚ Off map, west ✉ 1119 S Robertson Boulevard, West LA ☎ 310/275–4445, or 800/3–CARLYLE, fax 310/859–0496 🚌 220

CONESTOGA HOTEL

Old West-theme hotel; game room, babysitting, free shuttle to nearby Disneyland.

✚ Off map, southeast ✉ 1240 S Walnut Street, Anaheim ☎ 714/535–0300, or 800/824–5459, fax 714/491–8953 🍴 Restaurants 🚌 460

FIGUEROA HOTEL

Useful business hotel in central location. Also used as a convention centre.

✚ L8 ✉ 939 S Figueroa Street ☎ 213/627–8971, or 8000/421–9092, fax 213/689–0305 🚌 DASH C, F

FOUR POINTS HOTEL

A comfortable airport bargain with a 24-hour fitness room.

✚ Off map, southeast ✉ 9750 Airport Boulevard, LAX ☎ 310/645–4600, or 800/529–4683, fax 310/649–7047 🍴 Restaurant

HOLLYWOOD ROOSEVELT HOTEL

Refurbished Hollywood legend (▶ 53) with poolside cabana rooms.

✚ D1 ✉ 7000 Hollywood Boulevard, Hollywood ☎ 323/466–7000, or 800/950–7667, fax 323/462–8056 🍴 Good restaurant 🚌 1, 217

MALIBU COUNTRY INN

Romantic New England-style inn.

✚ Off map, west ✉ 6506 Westward Beach Road, Malibu ☎ 310/457–9622, or 800/386–6787, fax 310/457–1349 🍴 Continental breakfast included 🚌 434

PASADENA HOTEL

Turn-of-the-century bed-and-breakfast inn. No pool.

✚ Off map, northeast ✉ 76 N Fair Oaks Avenue, Pasadena ☎ 626/568–8172, or 800/653–8886, fax 626/793–6409 🚌 483, 485

THE STANDARD

A former retirement home now bustles with young guests and nightly DJ action.

✚ Off map, west ✉ 8300 Sunset Boulevard, West Hollywood ☎ 323/650–9090, fax 323/6502820 🍴 24-hour restaurant, bars 🚌 2, 3

UNIVERSAL CITY HILTON & TOWERS

Universal Studios packages, good family and business facilities.

✚ Off map, northwest ✉ 555 Universal Terrace Parkway, Universal City ☎ 818/506–2500, or 800/HILTONS, fax 818/509–2058 🍴 Restaurant 🚌 420, 424, 425

ZANE GREY PUEBLO HOTEL

The Western writer's 1926 pueblo-style home on Catalina Island.

✚ Off map, southwest ✉ 199 Chimes Tower Road, Avalon ☎ 310/510–0966, or 800/3–PUEBLO, fax 310/510–1340 🍴 Breakfast included

Bed and breakfast

Bed and breakfast and private home stays are popular alternatives to hotels. Bed & Breakfast California (☎ 800/872–4500; fax 415/696–1699; e-mail info@bbintl.com) offers reservations state wide for more than 300 historic homes, small inns and private homes providing bed-and-breakfast accommodation in charming rooms or separate apartments.

BUDGET ACCOMMODATION

Location

This is a major consideration when choosing a hotel in a sprawling city like LA. Most hotels listed are on the main east–west transport corridors between Downtown and the coast at Santa Monica. If your visit will last more than a few days, consider staying in a couple of different areas (Santa Monica and Hollywood, or Beverly Hills and Pasadena, for instance).

BANANA BUNGALOW HOLLYWOOD HOTEL/HOSTEL

Rooms and dorms; friendly, international atmosphere; free airport pick-up, beach and Disneyland shuttle, tour service, pool, cinema, a gym, laundry, kitchen, free parking.

✚ E1 ✉ 2775 W Cahuenga Boulevard, Hollywood ☎ 323/851–1129 or 800/4–HOSTEL, fax 323/851–1569 🍽 Restaurant 🚍 420

BAYSIDE HOTEL

Great position across from the beach and one block from Main Street.

✚ Off map, west ✉ 2001 Ocean Avenue, Santa Monica ☎ 310/396–6000, fax 310/396–1000 🍽 Restaurants nearby 🚍 4, 20, 22, 33, SM1, 7, 10

BEST WESTERN STOVALL'S INN

Large resort hotel close to Disneyland, mobbed with kids. Free shuttles to Disneyland and Anaheim, kid's menu, pool, Disney channel.

✚ Off map, southeast ✉ 1110 W Katella Avenue, Anaheim ☎ 714/778–1880, or 800/854–8175, fax 714/778–3805 🍽 Restaurants nearby 🚍 460

BEVONSHIRE LODGE MOTEL

Between Farmer's Market and the Beverly Center. Pool.

✚ Off map, west ✉ 7575 Beverly Boulevard, Midtown ☎ 323/936–6154, fax 323/934–6640 🍽 Restaurants nearby 🚍 14

CITY CENTER MOTEL

Small and quiet with a pool, west of the I–110/ Harbor Freeway downtown.

✚ L7 ✉ 1135 West 7th Street ☎ 213/628–7141, or 800/816–6889, fax 213/629–1064 🚍 DASH E

DESERT INN & SUITES

Well-equipped rooms and good facilities close to Disneyland.

✚ Off map, southeast ✉ 1600 S Harbor Boulevard, Anaheim ☎ 714/772–5050, or 800/433–5270, fax 714/778–2754 🍽 Restaurants nearby, breakfast included 🚍 460

ECONOLODGE HOLLYWOOD

Near Melrose Avenue and Hollywood.

✚ E3 ✉ 777 N Vine Street, Hollywood ☎ 323/463–5671, or 800/446–3916, fax 323/463–5675 🍽 Breakfast included 🚍 10, 11

HOSTELLING INTERNATIONAL

Good-size hostel close to the Santa Monica Pier. Courtyard, laundry, library, tours, activites. Some private rooms.

✚ Off map, west ✉ 1436 2nd Street, Santa Monica ☎ 310/393–9913, fax 310/393–1769 🚍 20, 22, 33, SM8

VENICE BEACH HOSTEL

Prime location near the ocean, a pool table and summer barbecues.

✚ Off map, west ✉ 151 Pacific Ave ☎ 310/452–3052, fax 310/821–3469 🚍 SM1, SM2, 333

LOS ANGELES
travel facts

ARRIVING & DEPARTING

Before you go

- British citizens require a valid 10-year passport to visit the US.
- A visa is required if 1) you are staying more than 90 days; 2) your trip is not a holiday or short business trip; 3) you have ever been refused a visa or admission to the US, or have been required to leave the US by the US Immigration and Naturalization Service; or 4) you do not have a return or onward ticket.
  Otherwise a Visa Waiver form is supplied by the airline.
- To apply for a visa contact the United States Embassy Visa Information Line, London ☎ 0891 200290
- No vaccinations are required unless you have come from or stopped in countries where there are epidemics.
- Travel insurance is not compulsory but it is strongly recommended. Comprehensive insurance, which should include medical coverage of at least $1,000,000, for a stay of up to one week will cost around £30 per person. Shop around travel agents and insurance companies for the best deal.

Climate

- LA is mild and temperate and sunshine and fair weather are pretty much guaranteed from May to October. Humidity ranges from 65 to 77 per cent. August and September can be unbearably hot and sticky and the smog is at its worst. The rainiest months are November to March.
- In summer, sea breezes temper the heat. The beach can be fogbound until mid-morning – be patient and it burns off.
- In winter, 70°F days can be interspersed with 50°F nights; you may need a sweater or jacket after dark.

Arriving by air

- Los Angeles International Airport (LAX) lies 17 miles southwest of Downtown. For information ☎ 310/646–5252
- Car rental companies provide free shuttles to their car parks from the ground transportation island outside the lower level baggage claim areas.
- Well-priced door-to-door shuttle bus services (24-hours) to all areas of the city, such as SuperShuttle ☎ 800/554–3146, also depart from here.
- The Metro Airport Service provides shuttle buses between all eight terminals (Shuttle A), and the remote car parks (Shuttle B and Shuttle C). Shuttle C serves the terminal for bus connections to the city.
- Depending on the traffic, a fare to Downtown or Hollywood will cost $35–45.

Arriving by bus

- LA's main Greyhound/ Trailways terminal is Downtown ⊠ 1716 East 7th Street. There are also terminals in Anaheim, Hollywood, Pasadena and Santa Monica.
- Information ☎ 800/231–2222

Arriving by train

- Visitors and commuters arrive at Union Station ⊠ 800 N Alameda Street, just north of Downtown, on the Metro Red Line and DASH shuttle bus routes.
- Information for Amtrak ☎ 800/872–7245

Customs regulations

- Duty-free allowances include 1 litre of alcoholic spirits or wine (no one under 21 may bring in alcohol), 200 cigarettes or 50 cigars (not Cuban) and up to $100-worth of gifts.

ESSENTIAL FACTS

Electricity

- The supply is 110 volts, 60 cycles AC current.
- US small appliances use flat two-prong plugs. European appliances require an adaptor.

Etiquette

- LA's dress code is casual. Men are rarely expected to don a jacket or tie to dine in the smartest restaurant in town.
- LA is hell for smokers. Smoking is banned in public buildings and also in restaurants and bars.
- Tipping is voluntary, but waiters expect 15–20 per cent, cab drivers 15 per cent, porters $1–2 per bag; and parking valets $1–2.

Liquor laws

- Bars can legally open at any time between 6AM and 2AM, though most open around 11AM and close around midnight (later on Fridays and Saturdays). Licensed restaurants can serve alcohol throughout their hours of business except between 2AM and 6AM. To buy or consume alcohol legally in California, you must be 21 or older. Youthful-looking patrons may well be asked to show proof of age.

Money matters

- The unit of currency is the US dollar (= 100 cents). Notes (bills) come in denominations of $1, $5, $10, $20, $50 and $100; coins are 50¢ (a half-dollar), 25¢ (a quarter), 10¢ (a dime), 5¢ (a nickel) and 1¢ (a penny),
- Nearly all banks have Automatic Teller Machines (ATMs), which accept cards registered in other countries that are linked to the Cirrus or Plus networks. Before leaving home, check which network your cards are linked to, and ensure your PIN number is valid in the US (four- and six-figure numbers are the norm).
- Credit cards are widely accepted.
- US dollar traveller's cheques function like cash in all but small shops; $20 and $50 denominations are the most useful. Don't bother trying to exchange these (or foreign currency) at banks.
- An 8.25 per cent sales tax is added to marked retail prices.

National holidays

- New Year's Day (1 Jan)
- Martin Luther King Day (third Mon Jan)
- President's Day (third Mon, Feb)
- Memorial Day (last Mon May)
- Independence Day (4 Jul)
- Labor Day (first Mon Sep)
- Columbus Day (second Mon Oct)
- Veterans' Day (11 Nov)
- Thanksgiving (fourth Thu Nov)
- Christmas Day (25 Dec)

Opening hours

- Shops: Mon–Sat 9 or 10 to 5 or 6. Department stores, shopping malls and shops in tourist areas keep longer hours and may also open on Sunday.

- Banks: Mon–Thu 10–4:30, Fri 10–6; savings banks and some banks open Saturday mornings.

Places of worship

- The phone book carries a comprehensive list.

Student travellers

- An International Student Identity Card (ISIC) brings reduced admission to many museums and attractions.
- Anyone aged under 21 is forbidden to buy alcohol and may be denied admission to some nightclubs.

Time differences

- Los Angeles is on Pacific Standard Time (US West Coast), three hours behind Eastern Standard Time in New York, eight hours behind the UK, nine hours behind Western Europe, 18 hours behind Sydney and two hours ahead of Hawaiian Standard Time.

Tourist offices

- Los Angeles Convention & Visitors Bureau ✉ 633 West 5th Street, Suite 6000, Los Angeles, CA 90071 ☎ 213/624–7300. There are two Visitor Information Centers: Downtown Los Angeles ✉ 685 Figueroa Street (between Wilshire and 7th Street), Los Angeles, CA 90017 🕘 Mon–Fri 8–5, Sat 8:30–5; Hollywood ✉ The Janes House, 6541 Hollywood Boulevard, Hollywood, CA 90028 🕘 Mon–Sat 9–5; a multi-lingual events hotline ☎ 213/689–8822 provides current information 24 hours a day.
- Long Beach Area Convention & Visitors Bureau ✉ One World Trade Center No. 300, Long Beach, CA 90831 ☎ 562/436–3645 or 800/452–7829

🕘 Mon–Fri 8–5

- Pasadena Convention & Visitors Bureau ✉ 171 S Los Robles Avenue, Pasadena, CA 91101 ☎ 626/795–9311 🕘 Mon–Fri 8–5, Sat 10–4
- Santa Monica Convention & Visitors Bureau ✉ 1400 Ocean Avenue, CA 90401–2117 ☎ 310/393–7593 🕘 Mon–Fri 9–5. Also Visitor Center ✉ 1400 Ocean Avenue ☎ 310/393–7593 🕘 Daily 10–4 (until 5 in summer)

PUBLIC TRANSPORT

- LA has a public transportation system operated by the Los Angeles County Metropolitan Transit Authority (MTA or Metro), though most locals and visitors prefer to drive.
- Buses provide the most extensive coverage of the city. Limited subway (Metro Red Line) and light rail (Metro Blue Line) services are due to be expanded rapidly in the next few years. The Metro Green Line parallels I–105 from Norwalk west to El Segundo.

Buses

- The DASH Downtown shuttle bus service operates within the downtown Financial District extending out to Exposition Park in the south, and north to Chinatown via Union Station and El Pueblo.
- The DASH operates every 5–15 minutes, Mon–Fri 6:30AM–6:30PM (some routes vary) for a flat fare of 25¢. Limited service at weekends. For more information ☎ 808–2273 (no area code required)
- The MTA bus services most useful to visitors are the main east–west routes Downtown to

Santa Monica, and north–south to the South Bay area.

- They operate daily 5AM–2AM, supposedly every 15 minutes, though services can be erratic. Otherwise, reduced-service night buses ply major routes.
- The flat fare is currently $1.35; transfers cost an additional 25¢. Have the correct change ready for the machine on boarding.

Metro rail services

- LA's Metro system is getting underway. Train services operate daily 5AM–11:20PM. The Metro Red Line subway extends from Union Station across Downtown and west on Wilshire Boulevard to Western Avenue. The new link to North Hollywood, with stops at Universal and Hollywood/Highland, is now open, with the Hollywood/Vine Street link still under construction.
- The Metro Blue Line between Downtown and Long Beach takes about 45 minutes, and services operate daily 5AM–10PM, with trains every 6–10 minutes in peak hours, 15 minutes at other times.

Schedule and map information

- Schedules and maps are available from the MTA ✉ ARCO Plaza, 515 S Flower Street (Level C), Los Angeles 🕐 Mon–Fri 7:30–3:30; ✉ 5301 Wilshire Boulevard 🕐 Mon–Fri 9–5; ✉ Union Station 🕐 Mon–Fri 6AM–6:30PM. Or ☎ 800–COMMUTE, give the operator your starting point and destination, and he/she will provide the best route on public transport 🕐 Mon–Fri 6AM–8:30PM; Sat–Sun 8–6

Taxis

- It is virtually impossible to hail

a taxi in the street, except (possibly) Downtown.
- Hotels and transport terminals are a good place to find a taxi, and restaurants will order one.
- Alternatively phone: Independent Cab Company ☎ 213/385–8294; LA Taxi ☎ 213/627–7000; or United Independent Taxis ☎ 323/653–5050

DRIVING

- The best way to get around LA is by car. Outside the weekday rush hour periods (7AM–9AM, 3PM–7PM), the freeway network is generally a fast, efficient way of getting across town. The freeways at first seem like five-lane racetracks, with overtaking on both sides and frequent lane-changing, but most visitors acclimatise quickly.

Car rental

- The main car rental companies have offices downtown as well as at LA International Airport. Alamo ☎ 800/327–9633; Avis ☎ 800/331–1212; Budget ☎ 800/227–7117; Dollar 800/800–4000; Hertz ☎ 800/654–3131; Bob Leech's ☎ 800/635–1240

Freeway driving

- Always plan your journey in advance using a freeway map (basic versions are supplied by car rental companies). Note the exit, the direction of travel, and the number and name of the freeway; remember that the same highway may go by a different name in each direction.
- The *Thomas Guide*, a comprehensive street guide, is available at good bookshops.

Regulations and speed limits

- Seat belts are required; children under 4 must be secured in a car seat.
- It is legal to turn right at a red light, after making a full stop, unless otherwise indicated.
- Pedestrians have right of way at crossings. Californians take this rule of the road seriously. Be sure to look for pedestrians before turning right on red.
- At four-way crossings without traffic lights, a courtesy code prevails; cars cross in order of arrival at the intersection.
- Freeway car pool lanes can be used by any car carrying the requisite number of passengers (generally two or three), indicated by signs posted at the freeway entrance.
- Unless otherwise posted, the speed limit is 55 or 65mph on urban freeways; 35mph on major thoroughfares; 25mph on residential and other streets.

MEDIA & COMMUNICATIONS

Newspapers and magazines

- LA's chief English-language daily newspaper is the *Los Angeles Times*, which covers international and local news.
- The free *LA Weekly* offers an excellent listings section with a comprehensive guide to clubs, music venues and arts events.
- Gay-orientated publications, such as *Frontiers* and *Edge* are widely available.

Post offices

- Minimum charges for sending a postcard or airmail letter (weighing up to an ounce) overseas are currently 55¢ and

$1 respectively. Stamps are available from post offices.
- Find the nearest post office in the phone book or ask at your hotel. Most open Mon–Sat 8:30 or 9 to 5 or 6, Sat until 1 or 2PM.

Radio and television

- LA's airwaves hum with everything from jazz to 'shock jocks' to Spanish and religious programmes. As a rule, the best talk radio is on the AM stations; the best music on FM.
- In addition to all the national network channels, many hotels have cable TV, pay-to-view movies and the Welcome Channel, a visitor information broadcasting service.

Telephones

- Local calls cost 35¢; insert coins then dial (no change given).
- LA has a number of local telephone codes. Some calls within the LA area require more than a 35¢ deposit. Dial the number and a recorded operator message gives the minimum deposit.
- The area code for Downtown Los Angeles is 213, which should not be dialled if calling from another 213 number. If dialling outside your area code, prefix the number with '1'. Other useful area codes: Beverly Hills and Santa Monica 310; Hollywood and the area immediately surrounding Downtown 323; Long Beach 562; Pasadena 626; San Fernando Valley 818.
- Calls from hotel room phones are much more expensive than those made on a public phone.
- Many businesses have toll-free numbers, prefixed 800 or 888. First dial '1' (ie '1–800').

EMERGENCIES

Emergency telephone numbers
- Fire, police or ambulance
  ☎ 911 (no money is required)

Consulates
- Australia ✉ 2049 Century Park East, 19th Floor ☎ 310/229–4800
- Denmark ✉ 10877 Wilshire Boulevard ☎ 310/443–2090
- Germany ✉ 6222 Wilshire Boulevard ☎ 323/930–2703
- Netherlands ✉ 11766 Wilshire Boulevard ☎ 310/268–1598
- New Zealand ✉ 12400 Wilshire Boulevard ☎ 310/207–1605
- Sweden ✉ 10880 Wilshire Boulevard ☎ 310/445–4008
- UK ✉ 11766 Wilshire Boulevard ☎ 310/477–3322

Lost property
- LA International Airport: each airline has its own lost property telephone number.
- Airport police ☎ 310/417 0440
- MTA (Metrobuses and Metrolink) ☎ 213/937 8920
- Otherwise call the relevant police precinct (addresses are listed in the phone book).

Medical treatment
- Many hotels can arrange for referrals to a local doctor or dentist. Or look under 'Physicians and Surgeons' or 'Dentists' in the *Yellow Pages*.
- Most city hospitals accept emergency cases. Those with well-equipped 24-hour emergency rooms include: Cedars-Sinai Medical Center Coveniently located for West Hollywood and Beverly Hills ✉ 8700 Beverly Boulevard, West Hollywood ☎ 310/855–5000 and Good Samaritan Hospital ✉ 616 S Witner Street ☎ 213/977–2121

Medicines
- Pharmacies are plentiful in LA; look in the *Yellow Pages*.
- Although many familiar drugs will be available (probably under unfamiliar names), if you are using medication regularly it is preferable to bring an adequate supply (see Customs Regulations).
- If you intend to buy prescription drugs in the US, bring a note from your doctor.

Sensible precautions
- Few visitors will ever see LA's high-crime areas. These include the notorious South-Central district, and East LA, which should be avoided.
- Venice Beach is also unpleasant after dark.
- Lone and women travellers should be careful and avoid unpeopled and unlit areas after dark.
- Always plan your journey in advance, and consult your car rental agency or hotel staff, or call your destination, to make sure of the freeway exit you want. The easiest way to wind up in the wrong neighbourhood is to take a wrong exit.
- Do not carry easily snatched bags and cameras.
- Carry only as much cash as you require.
- Most hotels provide a safe where you can leave valuables. Use it.
- Replacing a stolen passport begins with a visit or phone call to your consular office.
- Report any lost or stolen items to the nearest police precinct (see Lost Property) if you plan to make an insurance claim.

INDEX

INDEX

CityPack
Los Angeles

Written by   Emma Stanford

Edited, designed and produced by
    AA Publishing

Maps   © Automobile Association Developments Ltd 1997, 1999, 2000
Fold-out map   © RV Reise- und Verkehrsverlag Munich · Stuttgart
    © Cartography: GeoData

Distributed in the United Kingdom by AA Publishing, Norfolk House, Priestley Road, Basingstoke, Hampshire, RG24 9NY.

The contents of this publication are believed correct at the time of printing. Nevertheless, the publishers cannot be held responsible for any errors or omissions or for changes in the details given in this guide or for the consequences of any reliance on the information provided by the same. Assessments of attractions, hotels, restaurants and so forth are based upon the author's own personal experience and, therefore, descriptions given in this guide necessarily contain an element of subjective opinion which may not reflect the publishers' opinion or dictate a reader's own experiences on another occasion.
We have tried to ensure accuracy in this guide, but things do change and we would be grateful if readers would advise us of any inaccuracies they may encounter.

A CIP catalogue record for this book is available from the British Library.

ISBN 0 7495 1897 9

Published by AA Publishing (a trading name of Automobile Association Developments Limited, whose registered office is Norfolk House, Priestley Road, Basingstoke, Hampshire RG24 9NY. Registered number 1878835).

Colour separation by Daylight Colour Art Pte Ltd, Singapore
Printed and bound by Dai Nippon Printing Co (Hong Kong) Ltd.

Acknowledgements
The Automobile Association would like to thank the following photographers, libraries and associations for their assistance in the preparation of this book.
The Armand Hammer Foundation 27a; Gene Autry Western Heritage Museum 35b; Rob Holmes 55b; The Hulton Getty Picture Collection Ltd 12; The Huntington Library 46; J Paul Getty Museum 25a, 25b; Max Jordan 26a, 54; Angeles County Museum of Art 30; Photos courtesy of Los Angeles Convention & Visitors Bureau/ C 1995 5b, 6, 7, 13a, 31b; Museum of Neon Art 51(Lili Lakich); Norton Simon Art Foundation 45b; Petersen Automotive Museum 29a, 29b; Pictures Colour Library 24a, 37b; Rancho Los Alamitos 43; Tony Stone Images cover; © 1996 The Walt Disney Company 48. The remaining pictures are held in the Association's own library (AA Photo Library) and were taken by Phil Wood with the exception of pages 19, 36, 49b, 60 which were taken by Rob Holmes.

UPDATED BY *Julie Jares*
MANAGING EDITOR *Hilary Weston* INDEXER: *Marie Lorimer*

Titles in the CityPack series
- Amsterdam • Bangkok • Barcelona • Beijing • Berlin • Boston •
- Brussels & Bruges • Chicago • Dublin • Florence • Hong Kong • Lisbon •
- London • Los Angeles • Madrid • Miami • Montréal • Munich • New York •
- Paris • Prague • Rome • San Francisco • Seattle • Shanghai • Singapore •
- Sydney • Tokyo • Toronto • Venice • Vienna • Washington•